HARMONY IN PRACTICE

Anna Butterworth

The Associated Board of
the Royal Schools of Music

First published in 1999 by The Associated Board of the Royal Schools of Music (Publishing) Limited

Reprinted in 1999, 2001

© 1999 by The Associated Board of the Royal Schools of Music

ISBN 1 85472 833 4

AB 2462

Extracts from the following copyright works are reproduced with permission:

Bach: *371 Harmonized Chorales and 69 Chorale Melodies with figured bass* corrected, edited, and annotated by Albert Riemenschneider
© 1941 by G. Schirmer, Inc.
Reproduced by permission of G. Schirmer Ltd.

Elgar: *The Dreams of Gerontius*
© 1900 Novello & Co. Ltd
Reproduced by permission.

Elgar: *Enigma Variations*
© 1899 Novello & Co. Ltd
Reproduced by permission.

Fauré: *Après un rêve*
Reproduced by permission of Editions Hamelle, Paris/United Music Publishers Ltd.

Fauré: Pie Jesu, from *Requiem*
Reproduced by permission of Editions Hamelle, Paris/United Music Publishers Ltd.

Hindemith: *Traditional Harmony*
Reprinted by permission of Schott & Co. Ltd, London.

Leopold Mozart: *A Treatise on the Fundamental Principles of Violin Playing* translated by Editha Knocker (2nd edition, 1951)
Reprinted by permission of Oxford University Press.

Ravel: *Pavane pour une infante défunte*
Reproduced by permission of Editions Max Eschig, Paris/United Music Publishers Ltd.

Shostakovich: Piano Concerto No. 2, Op. 102
© 1957 by Anglo-Soviet Music Press Ltd (for Great Britain & British Commonwealth excluding Canada)
Reproduced by permission of Boosey & Hawkes Music Publishers Ltd.

Walton: 'Touch her soft lips and part', from *Henry V*
© Oxford University Press 1947
Reproduced by permission.

Cover design by Økvik Design
Text design and setting by Geoffrey Wadsley
Music origination by Michael Durnin
Printed in the United Kingdom by Halstan & Co. Ltd, Amersham, Bucks

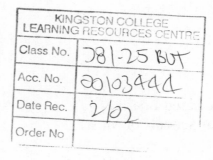

Contents

Author's Note

'Before beginning to play, the piece must be well looked at and considered. The character, tempo and kind of movement demanded by the piece must be sought out... Finally, in practising, every care must be taken to find and to render the affect which the composer wished to have brought out; and as sadness often alternates with joy, each must be carefully depicted according to its kind. In a word, all must be so played that the player himself be moved thereby.'

Leopold Mozart: Treatise on *The Fundamental Principles of Violin Playing* (1756)

As performers, we have to answer questions all the time about the music we are learning and playing. What does the score in front of us suggest in terms of musical sound and effect? What is the style, character and structure of the piece? What particular sound does the sum of the notes create through the combination of melody, harmony, rhythm and texture? What is the nature of the musical language which we as performers have to communicate to our listeners?

The more detailed our response to these questions and the greater our understanding of the musical language of the composers whose music we perform, the better our playing and singing will be. Awareness of matters of style and performance practice will add greatly to the sensitivity and validity of our music-making and enhance all our listening. In this way, a study of theoretical aspects of music, such as harmony, can contribute greatly to our practical abilities, and hence becomes very important in our development as musicians.

An Introduction to Tonal Harmony

'Harmony is a simple craft, based on a few rules of thumb derived from facts of history and acoustics – rules simple to learn and apply...'

Paul Hindemith: Preface to *Traditional Harmony* (1943)

'A simple craft'

Most of the music written in the so-called **tonal** era (*c.*1600–1900) is based on triads and organized in keys or around recognizable tonal centres. This includes such diverse music as a Bach keyboard prelude, a Mozart operatic aria and a Liszt symphonic poem.

The features which differentiate the styles of the Baroque, Classical and Romantic periods lie in the areas of melodic and harmonic decoration, in the variation of harmonic rhythm, in the range of the modulation[1], and in the textures[2] and timbres[3] of the music. However varied this music may seem, the **roots** are the same. Throughout this period, music is based on triads, built on the major and minor scales, and it moves in logical and satisfying progressions. Even though the music may appear complex, the craft of harmony is based upon comparatively simple principles.

Some 'facts of history'

Renaissance to Baroque: the development of tonality

The beginning of the seventeenth century saw some radical changes in musical style. Music from the earlier period of the Renaissance had favoured intricate part-writing or 'polyphony' – music in which our ears are focused on the progression of individual lines rather than on the resulting harmony. (A round or canon is a good example of such polyphonic music.) This was now rejected in favour of a simple and more direct form of expression, with a melodic line supported by harmonies built above the bass.

Such ideas were initiated by the Italian composer Giulio Caccini (*c.*1545–1618) and other members of the group of scholars and artists known as the **Camerata**. They were inspired by the ideals of ancient Greek theatre, and they devised a form of sung speech, called **recitative**, in which the words could be heard plainly. Monteverdi (1567–1643) created the first acknowledged opera in *L'Orfeo* (1607), using this so-called **stile recitativo** in a particularly effective way to recount the drama.

From modes to scales: music based in keys

This new 'vertical' trend in harmony coincided with another more gradual process in which the ancient 'modes'[4] were gradually replaced by the major and minor scale patterns on which tonal melody and harmony are based. Some modal features, especially the use of the flattened leading note and chord ♭VII, persisted throughout the seventeenth century and can be found, for example, in the music of Monteverdi, Purcell and Corelli. But by the early eighteenth century, music is clearly based in keys, with each chord in the key having a particular role to play in the harmonic order of things: for example, ii will move to V, V will move to I. Called **functional** harmony, this role is defined in the succession of chords known as 'the progression of 5ths' (*see* Chapter 9), which governs chord movement in the tonal period.

The Classical period: the assertion of tonality

The underlying principle of much music in the Classical period – for example the sonatas, symphonies, chamber ensembles and concertos of Haydn, Mozart and Beethoven – lay in a logical and ordered progression of keys expressed in the structure known as **sonata form**. A piece or a movement would first establish its key or tonal centre, by dwelling on the tonic and dominant notes and chords of the key. This was followed by excursions and modulations **away** from that tonal centre. Only when a return to the home key had been effected, with the tonal centre re-established, could a satisfactory conclusion occur.

The Romantic period: the preservation of tonality

Nineteenth-century composers sought to increase the effectiveness of musical expression in every possible way. Advances in technology and manufacture improved and made more reliable the piano and orchestral instruments. Composers made greater demands on performers, so that technical virtuosity was the order of the day. Their music was now written to be played with more extremes: faster and slower than before, with wider register of pitch, in greater dynamic detail and range (fff to pppp), and often at greater length than ever before. The *Symphonie Fantastique* by Berlioz demonstrates many of these features.

The actual music written ranged from the very simple to the highly complex and dramatic, with colourful harmony to match. Even so, with all these developments, the **basis** of the language remained unchanged: music was still built on triads in recognizable keys and followed certain well-used progressions.

The twentieth century: the breakdown of tonality

In the course of the twentieth century, radical changes occurred, with composers pursuing many different musical paths. Debussy, for example, adopted the whole-tone and pentatonic scales, and developed new harmonic techniques, such as writing in parallel movement[5] or using **chord clusters**[6]. Schoenberg devised a completely new system, later known as **serialism**, in which a strict arrangement of the twelve chromatic notes of the octave produced radically new 'harmony'. Nationalist[7] composers, such as Stravinsky, Bartók and Janáček, and more recently Messiaen and Copland, created sound worlds of which the rhythmic aspect has proved to be the most innovative and exciting characteristic. Other new areas of composition have included polytonality[8], electronically generated music, aleatoric music[9] and minimalism[10].

Despite all these developments, many composers, such as Shostakovich and Britten, have followed tonal principles to a varying degree. 'Pop' music, musicals and most film and TV music have also continued along tonal lines.

'Rules simple to learn and apply'

The main elements of tonal harmony will be explored in the course of this workbook, which aims to give students a secure knowledge of the basics of harmonic practice through singing, playing and completing appropriate exercises, and by listening to and noting musical examples.

Once a thorough knowledge of the chords – the tools of the trade – has been grasped, and the basis of chord progression has been understood, then the door to tonal harmony is opened. Students should then be able to tackle with confidence the more advanced work of the Associated Board Theory Grades 6 to 8 as well as the syllabuses of Advanced level and diploma work. They should also bring a greater understanding to bear on their practical music-making, discovering that harmony is, after all, a comparatively 'simple craft'.

1. *Modulation* See Chapters 12 and 13.
2. *Texture* The effect created by the combination of two or more instrumental and/or vocal lines.
3. *Timbre* Sound quality generated by instruments and/or voices.
4. *Modes* The different scales found in Western music before 1600. The modes in common use included the Dorian (equivalent to the white notes on a piano, from D to D), Phrygian (E to E), Mixolydian (G to G) and Aeolian (A to A). It will be seen that each mode is characterized by (*a*) a different sequence of tones and semitones, for example, the flattened supertonic of the Phrygian or the major 6th of the Dorian modes, and (*b*) by a flattened leading note.
5. *Parallel movement* See Chapter 4.

6. *Chord clusters* Chords comprising adjacent notes to create an aural effect rather than to serve a harmonic function.
7. *Nationalist composers* Composers who make use of the culture and folk music of their own country for inspiration.
8. *Polytonality* The simultaneous use of more than one key.
9. *Aleatoric* A term invented by Pierre Boulez to describe music that allows the performers a degree of freedom in what is played, rather than providing precise notation in a regular pulse.
10. *Minimalism* A compositional style that involves the intensive use of repeated rhythmic and melodic patterns. Steve Reich, Philip Glass, John Adams and other mainly American composers of the last quarter of the twentieth century are particularly associated with minimalism.

Chord Labelling

Two systems of chord labelling are used in this book. Each is explained fully in the chapters which follow, but this section may be useful for reference.

'Extended roman'

Of the various methods employed by musicians and teachers, 'extended roman' best identifies the **sound quality** of the chord (e.g. major) as well as its **function** within a key (e.g. chord V). In labelling correctly, the student will develop his awareness of the precise **sound** of each chord, even the difference between, for example, a **major**-sounding chord (IV) and a **minor**-sounding chord (iv).

- A capital (upper-case) letter indicates a major key: C = C major.
- A small (lower-case) letter indicates a minor key: c = C minor.
- A large (upper-case) roman numeral indicates a major chord (consisting of a major 3rd and a perfect 5th).
- A small (lower-case) roman numeral indicates a minor chord (consisting of a minor 3rd and a perfect 5th).

C: I   ii

- The numeral itself (I, II, III, etc.) indicates the degree of the scale on which the chord is built.
- The symbol ° placed next to a numeral indicates a chord, usually minor, that includes a diminished 5th.
- The symbol + placed next to a numeral indicates a chord, usually major, that includes an augmented 5th.

c: ii° III+

- Figures such as ^{7} and ^{9} indicate the interval read upwards from the bass, or a chord that includes that interval.

C: ii^7 V^9

- The letters a, b, c and d indicate, respectively, root position and first, second and third inversions. When a chord is in root position, it is usually indicated by the numeral alone, without the 'a'.

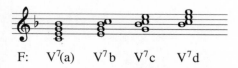

F: V^7(a) V^{7}b V^{7}c V^{7}d

- A ♯ or ♭ next to a roman numeral chromatically affects the root of the chord.

C: ♯iv°   c: ♭II   ♭IIb

Neapolitan 6th

- ᵈ⁷ indicates a diminished 7th from the bass of the chord.

c: viiᵈ⁷

- Aug. 6 (It.) (Ger.) (Fr.) indicates an augmented 6th chord in one of three variants: Italian, German or French.

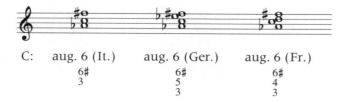

C: aug. 6 (It.)   aug. 6 (Ger.)   aug. 6 (Fr.)
            6♯   6♯   6♯
            3   5   4
                              3   3

Figured bass

This is a system developed in the Baroque period† (c.1600–1750) and still used today by continuo players on, for example, a harpsichord, organ or archlute. The figures are a kind of musical short-hand and indicate the intervals from the bass note, and hence the chords to be played, or 'realized', in performance.

Thus a triad in root position may be labelled $\frac{5}{3}$, because the notes a 3rd and 5th above the bass note are to be played.

C: 5
             3

The figuring does not indicate the position or scoring of the notes, which are left to the player.

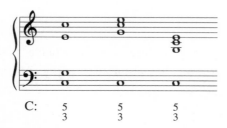

C: 5   5   5
        3   3   3

Since root position chords are so common, the figures $\frac{5}{3}$ were normally omitted in practice. In the cadential $\frac{6}{4}$ progression, however, the $\frac{5}{3}$ resolution is often indicated: $\frac{6}{4}$–$\frac{5}{3}$.

The following examples give the principal figures used, including inversions and dissonances. Bracketed figures were usually omitted.

† The musicologist, Hugo Riemann, identified the period 1600–1750 as the 'thorough-bass period'.

Chord inversions

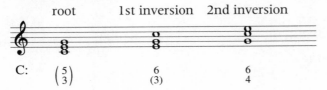

7th chords and inversions

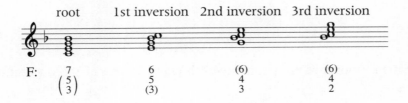

Accidentals

An accidental on its own applies to the third of the chord:

An accidental next to a figure alters chromatically the quality of that interval:

Suspension figurings

Indicate the movement of a part above the bass:

Figured bass will be used throughout this book, where appropriate. Keyboard players and lutenists are advised to become fluent readers of this system so that they are able to enjoy continuo work in Baroque music-making.

General Notes on the Use of this Book

Various areas, such as modulation and musical decoration, which involves accented passing notes, auxiliary notes and suspensions, for example, are mentioned relatively early on, since they are basic features of music. Such material is covered later in more detail.

Hymns, psalms and chorales have been used as examples and exercises in this book, since they are often familiar and provide straightforward examples of four-part tonal harmony. One should not underestimate their influence on Western art music; the chorale, in particular, sums up or encapsulates the harmonic language of the Baroque period.

Note that the key indication at the beginning of an exercise or example refers to the key *at that point* in the composition.

In many cases the initial exercises in the Exercise boxes have been worked for you. Continue with your working along the lines suggested.

In Part 1, note that the exercises involving the identification and labelling of triads consist of single chords; these are not intended to be chord progressions.

It is often suggested that you play the examples and exercises given. This is a valuable exercise, however slowly you may need to play! If you prefer, however, a teacher or friend could play them for you. The important aim is to be able to hear the dots on the page as soon as possible.

TRIADS
AND
CHORDS

Triads

CHAPTER 1

The building blocks of tonal harmony are the **triads** built on each degree of the major and minor scales. We therefore need to be able to locate, identify and describe them correctly and quickly in every key.

The label we give to each will reflect its **position** in the key in relation to the tonic (e.g. I, V, etc.), its **inversion** (e.g. root position, first inversion, etc.), and its **sound quality** (i.e. major, minor, diminished or augmented). We will examine all these features in Part 1 and there will be plenty of practice in writing and identifying triads and chords.

It is essential to hear the sound of each triad and its inversion. Always sing, hum or play all the triads and chords you write, in order to help develop the skill of reading a score 'in your head'.

There are various ways of labelling triads and chords. We could use numerals, figures below the staves or names, like 'G maj' or 'subdominant'. In this book we will in the main use a system called 'extended roman', which most fully reflects the nature of the chord and the notes found within it. This chapter sets out the basics of this system, which is explained in full on pages xiv–xv.

Triads in a major key in root position

Here are the triads built from each note of the scale of C major and numbered accordingly:

C: I   ii   iii   IV   V   vi   vii°

- These triads or three-note chords are made up of a root, a 3rd and a 5th.
- Large (upper-case) roman numerals indicate a major chord (*a*); small (lower-case) roman numerals a minor chord (*b*):

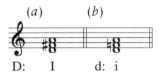

D: I   d: i

- A triad is major or minor depending on the type of 3rd involved. In ordinary major and minor chords, the 5th is always perfect:

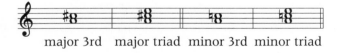

major 3rd   major triad   minor 3rd   minor triad

Augmented and diminished triads

- Notice that there is a small circle placed after the numeral for chord vii°. This indicates that the triad is **diminished**, i.e. the 5th of the chord is a diminished 5th above the root note.
- Finally, there is the **augmented** triad, formed when an augmented 5th is placed above the root note. We indicate this by adding a small plus sign after the numeral.

D: vii°   ii   ii°   D: I   I⁺   IV⁺   V⁺

◆ Because an augmented triad includes a major 3rd, it is represented, like the major triads, by an upper-case numeral; a diminished chord contains a minor 3rd, and so is represented by a lower-case numeral.

Exercises

1   Identify and label these triads, which may occur in major keys.

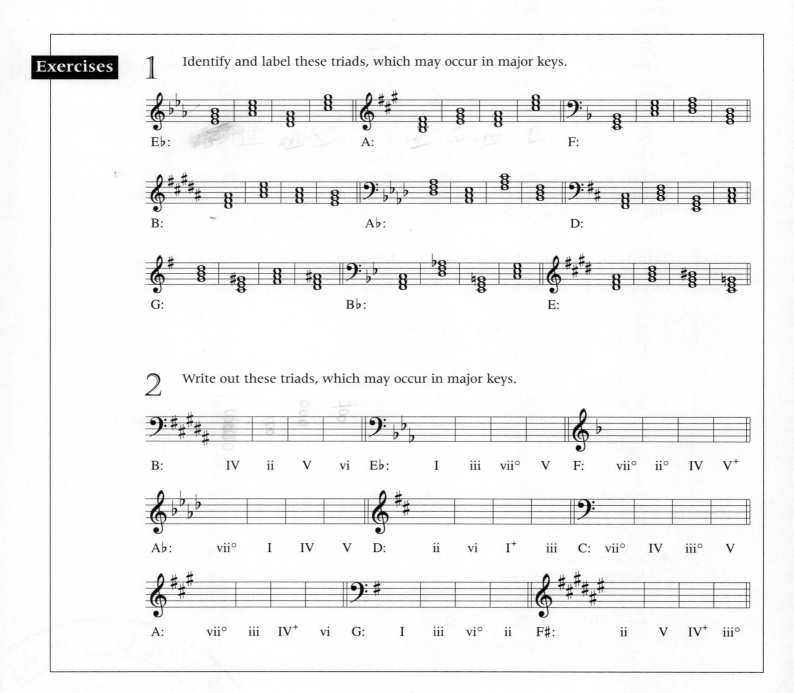

Eb: A: F:

B: Ab: D:

G: Bb: E:

2   Write out these triads, which may occur in major keys.

B: IV   ii   V   vi   Eb: I   iii   vii°   V   F: vii°   ii°   IV   V⁺

Ab: vii°   I   IV   V   D: ii   vi   I⁺   iii   C: vii°   IV   iii°   V

A: vii°   iii   IV⁺   vi   G: I   iii   vi°   ii   F#:   ii   V   IV⁺   iii°

Triads in a minor key in root position

◆ The minor scale can appear in various forms: harmonic, melodic ascending and melodic descending. (Another form, the natural minor scale, is known as the Aeolian mode; *see* p. xii, n. 4.)

◆ Because of this, each degree of the minor scale except the tonic has two triads which can be built from it, depending on whether the 6th and 7th degrees of the scale are lowered or raised.

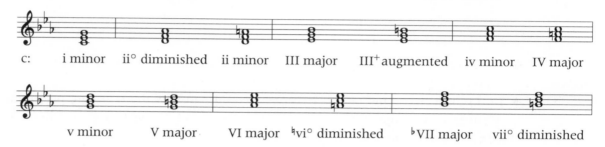

c: i minor   ii° diminished   ii minor   III major   III⁺augmented   iv minor   IV major

v minor   V major   VI major   ♮vi° diminished   ♭VII major   vii° diminished

◆ Normally, however, chord V is major in both major and minor keys, since its 3rd is the leading note of the key and is usually raised in order to confirm the key.

◆ The labelling assumes the harmonic minor scale to be the norm; when other scales are used the sound is reflected in the labelling.

Exercises

3   Identify and complete the labelling of these triads, which may occur in minor keys.

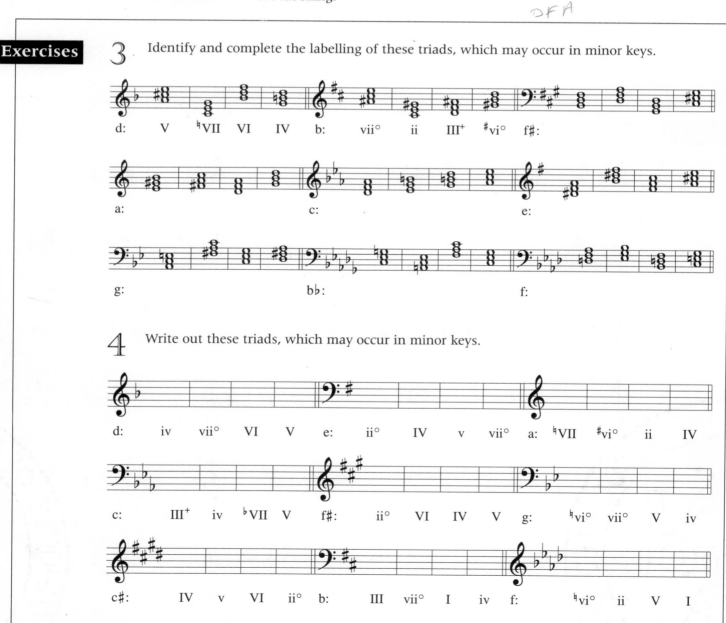

d: V   ♮VII   VI   IV   b: vii°   ii   III⁺   ♯vi°   f♯:

a: c: e:

g: b♭:   f:

4   Write out these triads, which may occur in minor keys.

d: iv   vii°   VI   V   e: ii°   IV   v   vii°   a: ♮VII   ♯vi°   ii   IV

c: III⁺   iv   ♭VII   V   f♯:   ii°   VI   IV   V   g: ♮vi°   vii°   V   iv

c♯:   IV   v   VI   ii°   b: III   vii°   I   iv   f: ♮vi°   ii   V   I

Triads in closed and open position

◆ The notes of a triad or chord may be close together (closed position) or spread further apart (open position):

C: closed position   open position

◆ The notes of a triad in open position may be placed in various ways, though the above example is probably the most usual spacing for a triad on one stave.

◆ Notice how the sound of a triad varies according to how the notes are placed on the stave and whether it is in open or closed position. The sound of the first triad below is quite 'muddy' compared with the other three examples.

G:

Exercises

5   Identify and label the following triads in closed position.

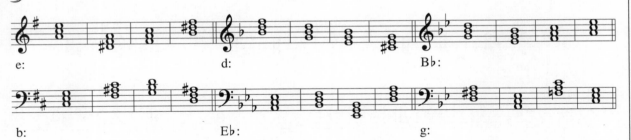

e: d: B♭:

b: E♭:   g:

6   Write out, without a key signature, the following triads in closed position. Include all the necessary accidentals.

D: I   vi   V   iii   g: iv   ii°   V   i   F: IV   ii   V   vi

A: ii   vi   V   vii°   C: ii   vii°   IV   V   E: IV   V   vii°   ii

d: ii°   V   VI   iv   E♭: I   IV   V   ii   b: i   VI   V   ii°

7 Identify and label the following triads in open position on one stave.

8 Identify and label the following triads, given without key signatures, in open position on two staves.

Naming triads

◆ We saw above that triads take their names from the degree of the scale on which they are formed. For example, the dominant triad is built on the 5th degree or dominant of the scale. Here are the names of all the triads.

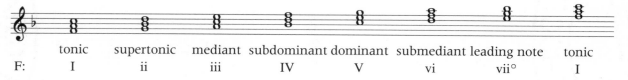

	tonic	supertonic	mediant	subdominant	dominant	submediant	leading note	tonic
F:	I	ii	iii	IV	V	vi	vii°	I

◆ Note that this system does not indicate that a triad is major or minor, diminished or augmented.

Exercise 9   Name the following triads to show their position in different keys.

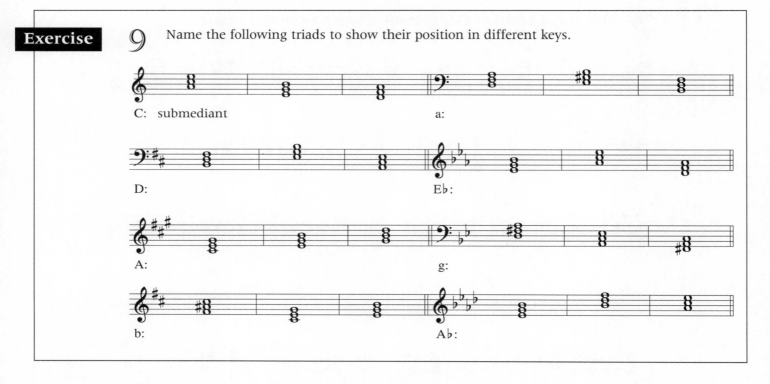

C: submediant   a:

D: Eb:

A: g:

b: Ab:

Primary and secondary triads

◆ Triads are divided into two groups – **primary** and **secondary**.

◆ The **primary** triads are the most important in the key and are built on the 1st, 5th and 4th degrees of the scale (the tonic, dominant and subdominant).

◆ They are the triads most often used, and between them can harmonize every note in the scale.

C: I   V   IV   a: i   V   iv

◆ The primary triads are also involved in forming the three principal **cadences**, which mark out phrase-endings, providing the essential breathing spaces in music (*see* Chapter 5).

◆ Chord viiº, though not strictly a primary triad, may be used as an alternative for chord V, as the notes of this chord are closely related to the notes of the dominant 7th chord (*see* Chapter 6).

Exercise 10   Write out the primary triads and the triad of chord viiº in the keys indicated, without key signatures. Include all the necessary accidentals.

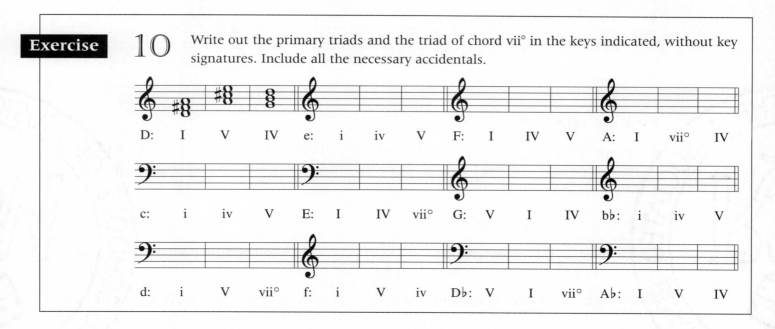

D: I   V   IV   e: i   iv   V   F: I   IV   V   A: I   viiº   IV

c: i   iv   V   E: I   IV   viiº   G: V   I   IV   bb: i   iv   V

d: i   V   viiº   f: i   V   iv   Db: V   I   viiº   Ab: I   V   IV

- The **secondary** triads are built on the 2nd, 3rd and 6th degrees of the scale.
- In a major key the triads built on the supertonic (ii), mediant (iii) and submediant (vi) are all minor.
- In a minor key, as we have seen, the character of the triad will depend on the type of minor scale used.

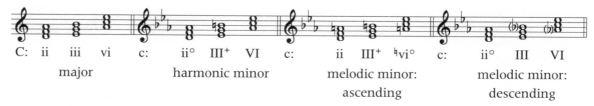

C: ii iii vi   c: ii° III⁺ VI   c: ii III⁺ ♮vi°   c: ii° III VI
major   harmonic minor   melodic minor: ascending   melodic minor: descending

Exercises

11 Write out, without key signatures, the secondary triads in the keys indicated. Include all the necessary accidentals.

b: ii° #vi° III   f: ii° III⁺ VI   A: vi ii iii

c#: ii° VI III⁺   d: ii° VI III   f#: ii° III VI

e: ii° VI III   bb: ii° VI III   Eb: iii vi ii

12 Write out the primary and secondary triads in open position as directed. Turn back to *Exercise 7* to see various examples of triads in open position on one stave.

g: V ii° VI   Eb: I IV iii   d: iv V VI

Bb: IV V I   c: iv VI ii   Eb: V vi I

A: IV ii V   a: iv V III⁺   f#: i V iv

G: iii V vi   b: iv V VI   e: VI V iv

13   Write out the primary and secondary triads in closed position in the following keys.
Remember that the leading note in chords V and vii° will need to be sharpened in the
minor key.

D: vii°   V   ii   B♭:   vi   IV   vii°   e: V   ii°   vii°

F: iii   V   ii   g: ii°   vii°   V   A: IV   vi   ii

c: V   iv   III⁺   f♯:   iv   V   i   E♭:   vi   V   ii

Inverting the Triad

CHAPTER 2

So far all the chords we have discussed in Chapter 1 have been in **root** position, i.e. the **root** of the triad appears in the **bass** part.

However, music which moved only in root position triads or chords would soon become uninteresting. **Inverting** the triad, i.e. putting the 3rd or 5th in the bass or lowest part, gives a wider choice of sounds to the composer.

Play and sing the following examples. At (*a*) (root position) the root of the triad is in the bass. At (*b*) (first inversion) the 3rd of the triad is in the bass, while at (*c*) (second inversion) the 5th is the lowest note. Notice how the sound of the triad varies according to whether it is in root position, first inversion or second inversion.

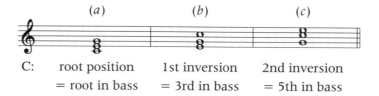

C: root position   1st inversion   2nd inversion
        = root in bass   = 3rd in bass   = 5th in bass

◆ Chord inversions can be indicated by letters (a, b, c) or numbers ($\frac{5}{3}$, $\frac{6}{3}$, $\frac{6}{4}$):

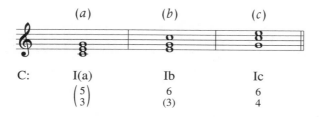

C: I(a)   Ib   Ic
        $\binom{5}{3}$ 6   6
                  (3)   4

In practice, the letter and numbers in brackets are usually omitted (*see also* Chord Labelling on p. xiv).

The numbers or figures we have just seen are examples of **figured bass**. This was a system used in the Baroque period (*c*.1600–1750) to indicate harmony. The figures are a kind of musical shorthand showing the intervals to be played above the given bass note. For example, $\frac{5}{3}$ indicates that the 5th and 3rd are to be played above the lowest note (the C in example (*a*) above).

Triads in first inversion

◆ First inversion triads are those in which the 3rd of the triad is the lowest note.
◆ The full figuring for a first inversion triad is $\frac{6}{3}$, though usually only the figure 6 is used.
◆ When a ♯ or ♮ is used to raise the leading note in chord vii°b in a minor key, a ♯ or ♮ is also placed after the figure 6:

d: vii°b   f: vii°b
        6♯   6♮

Exercises

14   Identify these triads in first inversion and label them with both numerals and letters and with figures. Check that your labelling matches the sound of the triad.

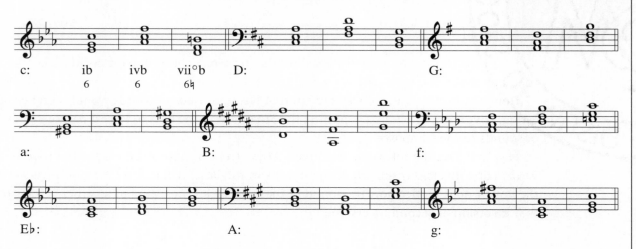

15   Practise writing out these triads in first inversion in various keys and clefs. Remember to sharpen the leading note where it appears in chords V and vii° in a minor key. First write out the triad in root position. Add the figuring.

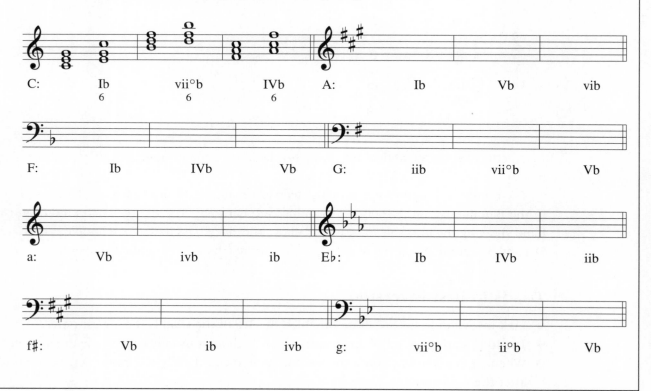

Triads in second inversion

◆ Triads in second inversion feature the 5th of the triad as the lowest note.
◆ The figuring for a second inversion chord is $\frac{6}{4}$.

Exercises

16 Identify these triads in second inversion and label them with both numerals and letters and with figures. Check that your labelling matches the sound of the triad.

17 Practise writing out these triads in second inversion without key signatures. Remember that the 5th of the triad is in the bass and check all accidentals. Write out the triad in root position first.

Here now is some revision of the work you have done so far on triads, using music extracts.

Exercise 18   In each of the following extracts label the triads marked with an asterisk (*).

◆ Note that the triads in the key of the passage to be worked have been printed alongside each of the extracts. You will find such preparatory work extremely useful in attempting an exercise, and you should adopt this procedure wherever appropriate.

◆ Notice also that sometimes not all of the notes of the triad are included in a chord. The 5th is often omitted. Generally a chord should contain a 3rd, although some of the extracts below end simply with the key note, which is enough to imply the tonic chord.

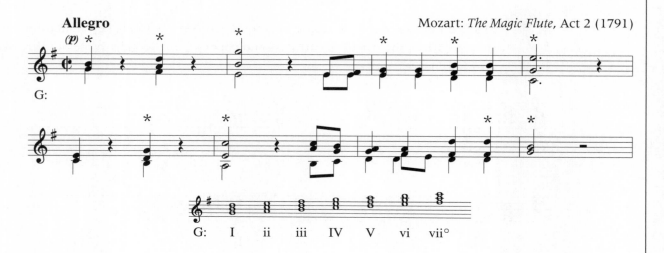

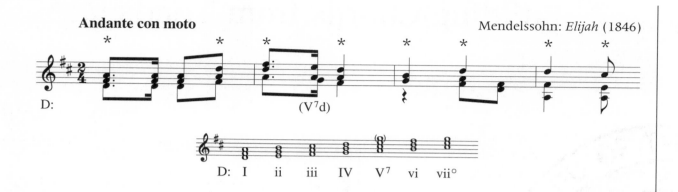

Andante con moto   Mendelssohn: *Elijah* (1846)

D: (V⁷d)

D: I   ii   iii   IV   V⁷   vi   vii°

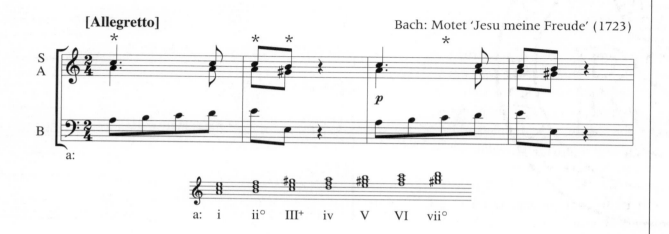

[Allegretto]   Bach: Motet 'Jesu meine Freude' (1723)

a:

a: i   ii°   III⁺   iv   V   VI   vii°

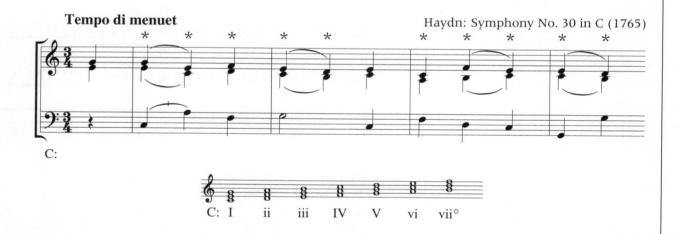

Tempo di menuet   Haydn: Symphony No. 30 in C (1765)

C:

C: I   ii   iii   IV   V   vi   vii°

Building Chords from Triads

CHAPTER 3

We have now looked in detail at the way triads are constructed and you will be familiar with the labelling and figuring of them. In this chapter we shall examine how they are extended into chords.

◆ Chords are normally constructed from the notes of the triads in a key, and labelled in the same way. In practice any number of notes in the triad may be doubled and placed in any order and at any pitch above the bass.

In all the examples below, the chord marked with an asterisk is chord I in C major. As you can see, 'harmony' is not restricted to hymn tunes or song accompaniments!

Haydn: *The Creation* (1796–8)

C: 'And there was light'   * I

Bach: Prelude in C, from *The Well-Tempered Clavier*, Bk 1 No. 1 (1722)

C: *I_____ *I_____

*I_____ *I_____

Allegro ma non troppo Schubert: String Quintet in C (1828)

C: *I_____ *I_____

Debussy: 'La cathédrale engloutie', from *Préludes*, Bk 1 (1910)

Sonore sans dureté

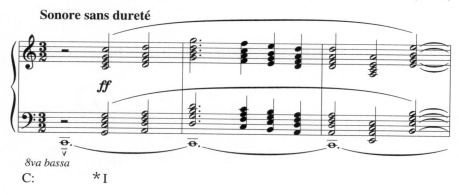

8va bassa

C: *I

Some chord **progressions** may suggest cadences, just as individual words joined together make sense in sentences and paragraphs. (Both processes have developed over many years and follow clearly defined principles.) We shall look at the way chords move and relate to each other in the tonal period in Part 2. In this chapter we shall see how chords are constructed and practise writing and identifying them in various keys.

Writing in four parts

In the tonal period four-part writing became the norm for much music, such as:
- the many Baroque ensembles of two violins, viola and bass line;
- the vocal music of Bach and Handel;
- the string section of the Classical orchestra of Haydn and Mozart;
- the string quartet.

Handel: *Messiah* (1742)

Mozart: Piano Concerto in A, K488 (1786)

Haydn: String Quartet in C, Op. 76 No. 3 (*c.*1799)

Much harmony is written for voices in four parts with soprano, alto, tenor and bass voices (usually abbreviated to SATB) covering the vocal range. You will find this choral layout in oratorio and opera choruses and vocal quartets, as well as in hymns and chorales. It is important to be able to score harmony for a four-part vocal texture, as an understanding of the principles of this will lead to good part-writing in many other musical contexts.

◆ Good harmony strikes a balance between the vertical progression of chords on the one hand, and the linear movement of individual parts within the texture on the other.

Here are some useful hints for writing in four parts.

Vocal ranges

The normal vocal ranges of the four voices are given below, though composers have often written outside these ranges, especially in dramatic situations:

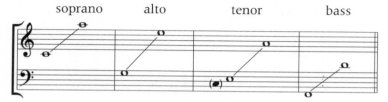

◆ Keep the tenor part in the region of middle C.

◆ Any large gap between the parts should occur between the tenor and bass parts.

◆ 3rds low down in the texture sound 'muddy'.

◆ Keep within the 'working' vocal ranges given above, as this will help your part-writing and ensure it is practicable. As you gain more confidence in your writing, you may extend the ranges slightly in particular instances.

Note doubling

◆ It follows that in a four-part texture one of the notes of the triad must appear twice, or be 'doubled', unless a 7th or other additions to the triad are included (*see* Chapter 6). If you follow the points below you will achieve the right sound, but you should always test this on the keyboard.

• You may double the **root** of the triad, except in chord vii°, where it is the leading note; in four-part harmony this 'strong' note in the key tends not to sound well if doubled. In addition, doubling the leading note would require consecutive resolution between two parts, since the leading note resolves to the tonic, and it is one of the few 'rules' of part-writing to avoid consecutive movement (*see* Chapter 4).

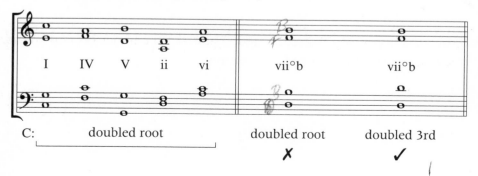

- The **3rd** of the chord is normally included. The **doubling** of the major 3rd produces a characteristic, rich sound. Although it was doubled extensively by Bach (for example in his chorales) it is best at this stage to double the major 3rd only when it is two octaves apart. However, it should **not** be doubled if it is the leading note (in chord V). Doubling minor 3rds is acceptable.

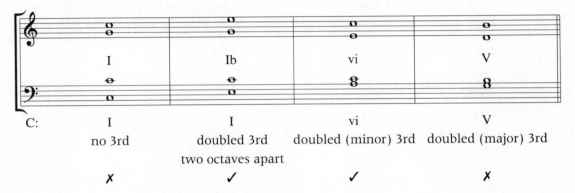

- The **5th** may be omitted or doubled; either sound is quite acceptable.

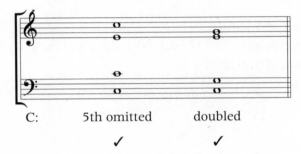

Four-part chords in root position

- In root position triads or chords, the lowest or root note of the triad appears in the lowest or bass part.
- In figured bass the full figuring for a root position chord is $\frac{5}{3}$ though, as we have seen, both numerals are usually omitted in practice.
- Where a chord contains an altered 3rd, often the sharpened leading note in a minor key, it is indicated in figured bass by the appropriate accidental – ♯, ♮ or ♭ – placed by itself.

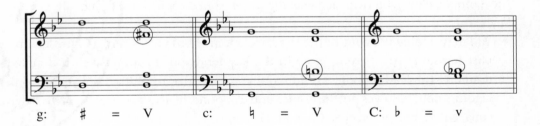

- Diminished triads (vii° in a major key, and ii° and vii° in a minor key) do not normally occur in root position. Use these chords in first inversion.

Exercises 19 Play and listen to the sounds of these examples then write out the root position chords as indicated. This will give you practice in extending triads into four-part chords. Use the staves provided to write out the triads in the keys of the exercises, as shown in the first examples. In minor keys build your triads on the **harmonic** minor scale, but remember that the melodic minor scale may also occur, in which case the **quality** of the triads (major, minor, etc.) will be changed (*see* p. 5). This should be indicated in the chord label.

Normally you will need to sharpen the leading note in chord V in a minor key, since it is not in the key signature.

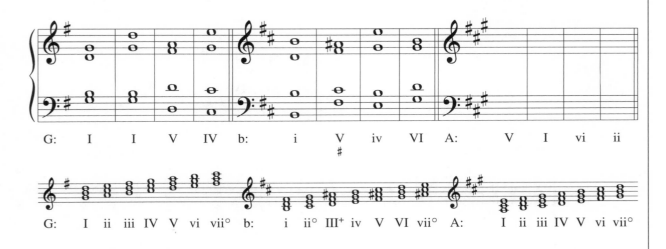

G: I   I   V   IV   b: i   V   iv   VI   A: V   I   vi   ii
                                  #

G: I   ii   iii   IV   V   vi   vii°   b: i   ii°   III⁺   iv   V   VI   vii°   A: I   ii   iii   IV   V   vi   vii°

d: i   V   VI   iv   a: VI   i   V   III⁺   F: ii   IV   V   I
         #   #

d: i   ii°   III⁺   iv   V   VI   vii°   a: i   ii°   III⁺   iv   V   VI   vii°   F:

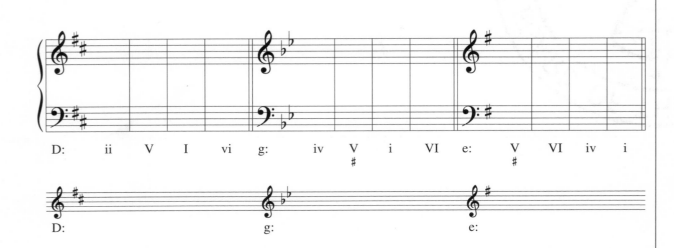

D: ii   V   I   vi   g: iv   V   i   VI   e: V   VI   iv   i
                                  #   #

D: g: e:

20   Identify the chords marked with an asterisk in the extracts below. Label them with roman numerals.

'Old Hundredth'

French Psalter (1551)

'Es ist ein' Ros''

German, 15th century
arranged Praetorius (c.1571–1621)

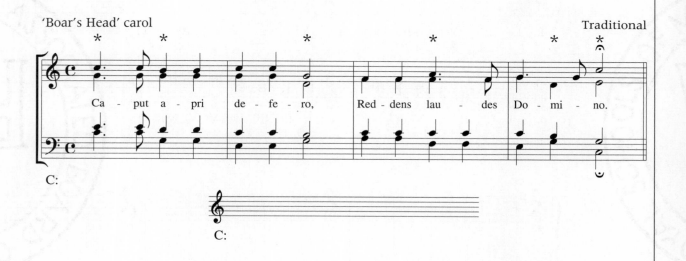

'Boar's Head' carol

Traditional

Uses of chords in root position

◆ Root position chords create a very stable effect in music, which is why they form the principal resting-places or cadences, notably the perfect cadence, V–I. (We will look in more detail at cadences in Chapter 5.) In the following extract all the chords except one are in root position; note the strong effect they create:

Welsh melody

G: I   IV   ii   V   Ib   IV   V   I

Exercise 21   Play through the extracts given in *Exercise 20*, listening especially to the bass line and to the feeling of stability which results from the root position chords.

Four-part chords in first inversion

◆ In figured bass the full figuring for a first inversion chord is $\frac{6}{3}$ though, as we have seen, in practice the 3 was usually omitted.

◆ In a minor key the sharpened leading note in vii°b is expressed by the appropriate accidental (♮ or ♯) placed after the figure (the 6):

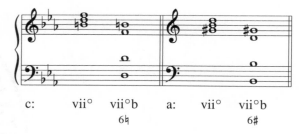

c: vii°   vii°b   a: vii°   vii°b
                 6♮   6♯

◆ Note that an accidental placed next to the **bass** note on the stave is not reflected in the figuring (last chord of music below):

c: 6♮   6   6♭   6   6

◆ The sound of a first inversion chord is more satisfactory if you double the root or 5th, rather than the bass note. This is especially true in a major chord, as you would otherwise be doubling the major 3rd, which always needs care (*see* p. 20).

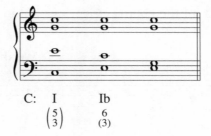

C: I   Ib
      $\binom{5}{3}$ 6
                   (3)

◆ Note, however, that in chord vii°b you should double the 3rd rather than the leading note or 5th, as to double either of these notes would emphasize the tritone outline of this chord, which is a less satisfactory sound.

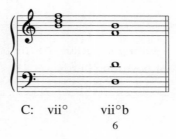

C: vii°   vii°b
                   6

Exercises

22 Write out the chords as indicated in first inversion. Add figuring. Keep an eye on the chord spacing. Use the staves provided to write out the triads in the keys of the exercises.
Remember to sharpen the leading note in a minor key. This occurs in chords V and vii°.

23 Play through the chords you have written in *Exercise 22* and familiarize yourself with the sound of them.

24   Identify the chords marked with an asterisk in the extract below. Label them with roman numerals and with figured bass. It may help to write out the triads in the key of the extract.

        Play the example, listening especially to the bass line.

Scottish Psalter (1635)

Uses of chords in first inversion

◆ Chords in first inversion act as a foil and contrast to the stronger root position chords, and always seem to progress towards them. Their role is a transitional one between cadences or points of repose, which are normally in root position.

Exercise 25   In the following extract identify and label the asterisked chords, which are in first inversion, and note their position in the phrase.

Handel: *Leçon* No. 1 in Bb† (*c*.1720)

† This is the theme used by Brahms in his *Variations on a theme by Handel* Op. 24 for piano.

◆ A characteristic sound of Renaissance music was the smooth progression of first inversion chords, called **fauxbourdon**:

Palestrina: Mass *Aeterna Christi munera* (1590)

◆ We also hear this in the Baroque period and beyond:

Corelli: Trio Sonata, Op. 1 No. 2 (1683)

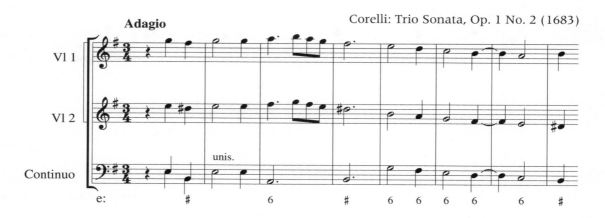

Exercise   26   Label the chords marked with an asterisk in these extracts and note the progression of the first inversion chords.

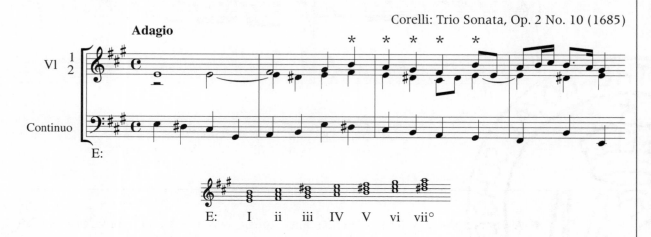

Corelli: Trio Sonata, Op. 2 No. 10 (1685)

E: I   ii   iii   IV   V   vi   vii°

Handel: Suite No. 3 in D minor (1720)

d: i   ii°   III⁺   iv   V   VI   vii°

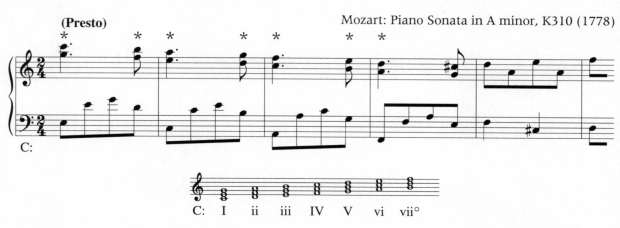

Mozart: Piano Sonata in A minor, K310 (1778)

C: I   ii   iii   IV   V   vi   vii°

Four-part chords in second inversion

You will not meet second inversion chords so much as those in root and first inversion. However, the examples and exercises in this section will help you to recognize them quickly. As before, listen to the **sound** of the chord as you play the various examples.

◆ In figured bass the second inversion chord is figured as $\frac{6}{4}$.

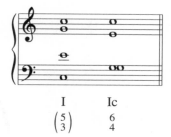

- ◆ In second inversion chords it is the bass note or 5th of the triad which is normally doubled.
- ◆ The 4th of the $\frac{6}{4}$ is rarely doubled, since it is a **dissonance** above the bass and requires resolution down to the 3rd (*see* p. 202). Two 4ths would therefore move in consecutive octaves and the avoidance of consecutive 5ths and octaves in the part-writing of chord progressions is one of the few 'rules' in tonal harmony (*see* Chapter 4).

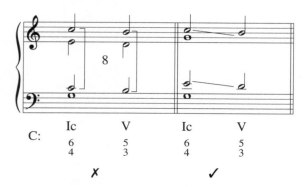

- ◆ Doubling the 6th similarly requires care to avoid consecutive movement, and for this reason it is best to double only the 5th, or bass note, as in these examples:

- ◆ In practice, only Ic, Vc and IVc are met on a regular basis.

Exercises   *27*   Write out the $^6_4$ chords indicated. Remember to double the bass note or 5th of the triad.

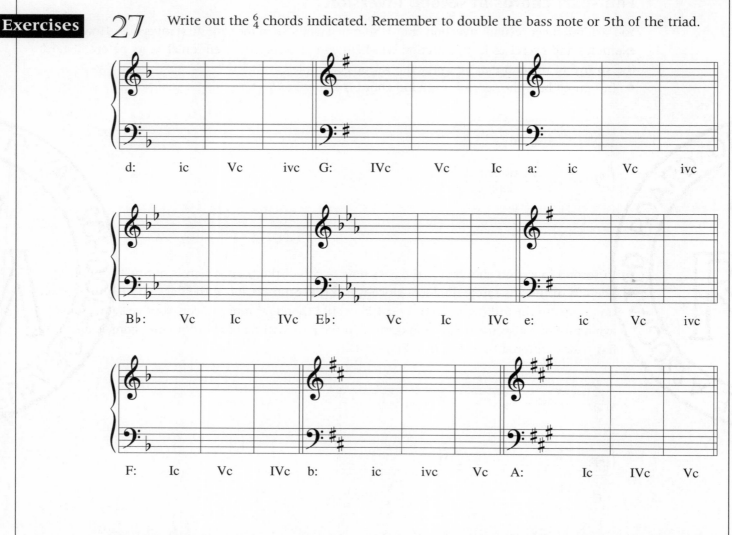

d: ic   Vc   ivc   G: IVc   Vc   Ic   a: ic   Vc   ivc

B♭:   Vc   Ic   IVc   E♭:   Vc   Ic   IVc   e: ic   Vc   ivc

F: Ic   Vc   IVc   b: ic   ivc   Vc   A: Ic   IVc   Vc

28   Play through the chords you have written in *Exercise 27* and familiarize yourself with the sound of them.

Uses of chords in second inversion

Progressions involving the $^6_4$ chord will be given in Chapter 7.

PART 2

SIMPLE
PROGRESSIONS

Some 'Rules' to Follow

CHAPTER 4

So far we have established that composers in the tonal period wrote harmony based on chords derived from triads in recognizable keys or tonal centres. This chapter is concerned with the way composers used these chords to create the musical language that we associate with the tonal period.

The various practices which they followed, and which characterized their music, are usually summarized for students in the 'dos' and 'don'ts' of harmony, the 'rules'. There are, however, very few **inflexible** rules in tonal harmony, and all of these were broken from time to time by composers. In the pages which follow we shall be noting what was good practice, and what was avoided because it was considered poor practice. Most composers received strict training in good practice and you should aim to adopt the same principles and follow the same rules as they did in order to understand their language and find the correct sound of the style.

For the sake of completeness, the most important 'rules' have been included in this chapter. You should note the 'consecutive rule', in particular, as you start to write harmony.

The 'consecutive rule'

◆ Perhaps the most important 'rule' of tonal harmony is the strict avoidance of consecutive or parallel octaves and 5ths between moving parts.[†] Note the consecutive octaves and 5ths in the following example:

This practice was avoided from the end of the thirteenth century and became a firmly established rule of Renaissance music. The English composer Thomas Morley (1557/8–1602), who wrote one of the first textbooks on music, *A Plaine and Easie Introduction to Practicall Musicke* (1597), declared, 'I do utterly condemn it as being expressly against the principles of our art'. Morley also emphasizes that the great composers of his time, including 'Mr Byrd', would not write in consecutives, blaming others for any mistakes: 'but if you chance to find any such things in their works you may be bold to impute it to the oversight of the copiers'.

◆ The most serious consecutives are those which occur between the outer parts, that is, between the treble (or soprano) and bass. A check should be made on these two parts before filling in the inner voices.

Morley's rules on consecutives continued to be recognized throughout the tonal period and consecutives are **not** generally found in the music of Bach, Beethoven, Brahms and other composers of this era. It is only in the twentieth century that this rule has been relaxed. One of the radical innovations of the French impressionist composer Claude Debussy in the early years of the twentieth century was to introduce consecutive movement, in 7ths and 9ths as well as 5ths and octaves, into his part-writing. This technique contributed to the characteristic new sound of his music. Here is a well-known example:

[†] Though, in the interests of sonority in piano writing, a composer may double a bass line in octaves.

Debussy: 'La cathédrale engloutie', from *Préludes*, Bk 1 (1910)

Profondément calme (*Dans une brume doucement sonore*)

◆ The only thorough method of checking for consecutives is to count the interval between each part. Adjacent 5ths and octaves will reveal the consecutives.

(BS)	Bass to Soprano	8		5	–	5	–	5	3	8	–	8	3	8
(BT)	Bass to Tenor	5	–	5	–	5			3	8	5	–	5	8	5
(BA)	Bass to Alto	3		3		3			8	5	3		3	8	3
(TA)	Tenor to Alto	6		6		6			6	5	6		6	8	6
(TS)	Tenor to Soprano	4		8	–	8			3	3	4		4	3	4
(AS)	Alto to Soprano	6		3		3			5	6	6		6	3	6

◆ Although this is a laborious method, it is advisable in order to establish a system and habit of checking. As each chord is completed it should be checked against the previous one (the process may be done mentally, but should still be systematic). In time the eye will become familiar with the 'shape' of consecutive intervals.

◆ Note the following points:
   • You should check particularly those parts that move in the same direction. Aim for movement in contrary motion, particularly between the outer parts.
   • However, even in contrary motion consecutive 5ths and octaves are considered unacceptable:

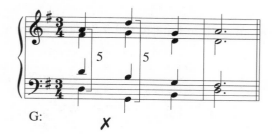

- The **repetition** of the interval of an octave or 5th is acceptable – 'consecutives' only involve movement:

'Adeste fideles'

- The interval of a perfect 5th to a diminished 5th (or vice versa) is acceptable in the **inner** parts but not between the bass and another part:

'Exposed' octaves or 5ths

◆ Composers have tended **not** to include 'exposed' octaves or 5ths in their part-writing. These occur when the outer or 'exposed' parts move in the same direction to an octave or 5th, with a jump in the melody line:

◆ Note that it is the leap in the upper part which contributes to the unsatisfactory nature of this progression; movement in the lower part is always acceptable:

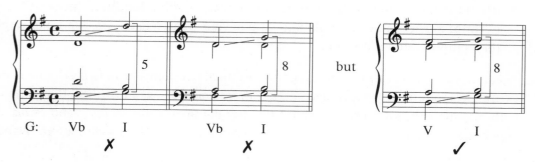

Exercise 29   Identify the consecutive movement with red ink in the following adapted harmonizations of hymn tunes.

'Old Hundredth'   Adapted from Dowland (1592)

Adapted from Day's Psalter (1563)

Adapted from Ravenscroft's Psalter (1621)

The resolution of dissonances and other notes of motion†

We can hear that certain notes, like leading notes, contain various 'pulls' which require resolution in certain directions. In the following progression, for example, the leading note moves to the tonic and the 7th, which we will examine in Chapter 6, resolves down by step:

C:

◆ It is important to follow this 'natural' movement of **voice-leading**, since this is a primary factor in **tonal** music, and you should take care in your written exercises that notes resolve or move in the 'right' or natural direction.

Again, it was in the early twentieth century, as tonal harmony began to break down and several new, exciting compositional styles emerged, that these practices were modified. Composers experimented with altering the **function** of a chord like the dominant 7th; in his piano *Prélude* 'La cathédrale engloutie', for example, Debussy wrote a sequence of dominant 7ths without resolving any of them:

† *See* Chapter 14, p. 202.

Debussy: 'La cathédrale engloutie', from *Préludes*, Bk 1 (1910)

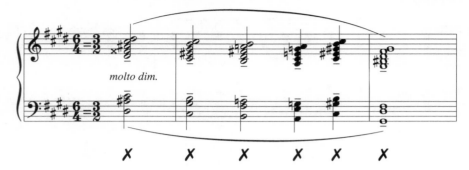

Note doubling and the movement of parts in the texture

◆ It follows that those notes that need to move in a certain direction are generally **not** doubled, since if they were consecutive movement would result.

◆ This applies to leading notes:

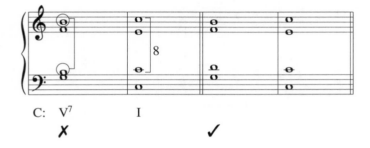

◆ all 7ths added to a chord, including dominant and diminished 7ths (*see* Chapter 6, p. 62):

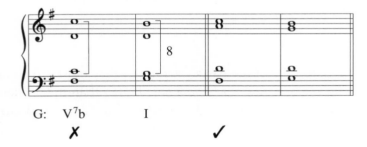

◆ all dissonances, including suspensions and appoggiaturas (*see* Chapter 5, p. 49):

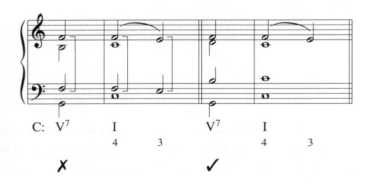

A few textbooks have stated that you should avoid doubling major 3rds. It is true that **some** doubled major 3rds will sound poor, but there are many examples of them in tonal music. Composers, notably Beethoven, sometimes opt to double the major 3rd, as well as doubling at the octave, in a texture to **create a special sonority**. Listen to the opening bars of his Piano Concerto No. 4:

Beethoven: Piano Concerto in G, Op. 58 (1805–6)

Here is an extract from a Bach chorale which contains several instances of doubled 3rds. Notice how they are often the result of parts moving in contrary motion and that their effect is reduced by the quaver movement. Perhaps the most characteristic spacing places them two octaves apart, as in the first example marked (*a*).

◆ If you double the major 3rd, you need to be satisfied with the sound in its context. Listen to the effect it creates; it may be that a doubled root or 5th would sound better.

Overlapping of parts

Notice how in the following extract some of the parts 'overlap' as they move from chord to chord. In the second chord, for example, the bass has moved to a note higher than the previous tenor note; in the fifth chord the soprano has moved below the previous alto note (and there are other examples):

◆ It is better **not** to overlap parts in the early stages of working harmony. The result can be clumsy and the part-writing inelegant. However, you will notice that Bach frequently overlaps the voice parts (A, T and B) in his chorale harmonizations, usually in the interest of a melodic line. See the expressive tenor part in the following example:

---

† R refers to the number in A. Riemenschneider, *371 Harmonized Chorales and 69 Chorale Melodies with Figured Bass by J. S. Bach* (Schirmer, 1941).

R50   Bach: Chorale

F:

◆ You will also find that tenor and bass parts sometimes appear to overlap. The chorales would have been accompanied by an organ with a coupler that would double the bass line an octave below, so that it remained the true bass of the harmony.

R59   Bach: Chorale

B♭:

Cross- (false) relations

One characteristic sound that arises out of a peculiarity of part-writing is the so-called cross-relation. When ascending and descending lines both include the leading note, often one is sharpened and one is not. When sounded close together or simultaneously the semitone 'clash' is particularly striking. The effect was used in particular by English composers of the Renaissance, such as Byrd and Tallis, and its frequent occurrence at cadences gave rise to the term 'English' cadence. Cross-relations were usually used in association with word-painting, heightening the meaning of the text through the dissonance involved. Though the sound is found mostly in modal music, you may well encounter it in tonal music as well. Here are some characteristic examples:

Tallis: 'O nata lux' (1575)

g:

Weelkes: 'O care, thou wilt despatch me' (1600)

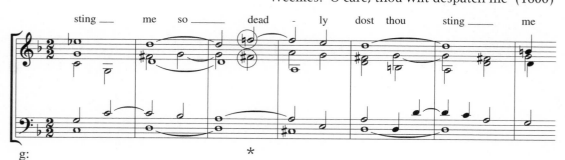

g:

You will not find this dissonance very often after the time of Purcell (1659–95), and the following example from Mozart is an infrequent occurrence in tonal music, retained for expressive purposes.

Mozart: *Sinfonia Concertante* for violin and viola, K364

◆ Writing cross-relations should normally be avoided. If possible, an accidental should be altered in the same part to avoid cross-relations in adjacent chords. However, this is not always possible, and you will find numerous examples in Bach's chorale harmonizations, especially when a change of key involves a new accidental.

R109   Bach: Chorale

Summary

◆ The strict avoidance of consecutives and the proper resolution of dissonances and other notes of motion are basic principles of the style.
◆ Adherence to the other points made in this chapter will help you produce satisfactory harmonic progressions and good part-writing, and it is wise to follow these guidelines as you begin to write tonal harmony.
◆ However, the practices of voice-leading or texture were not inflexible and we have already seen how composers adapted them to their own needs.
◆ Your ear must be the judge as to whether the **sound** is acceptable or stylistic in the context in which it appears.

Harmonizing Melodies – the Cadential Progressions

From earliest times, as far as we can tell, musicians added a variety of accompaniments to their songs and dances. The simplest may have consisted of basic percussion patterns or a drone bass. More sophisticated instruments such as lutes and harps were able to add **harmony**. Frequent **cadence** points occurring in the course of the music attracted certain strong chord **progressions**. Cadence progressions involve the strongest harmonies we shall find in tonal music, while the cadences themselves are the essential breathing spaces in the melody lines, and function like punctuation marks.

The more we listen to or play music, the more we realize that chords do not exist as isolated sounds but relate to each other in established progressions.

Here are examples of the four principal cadences:

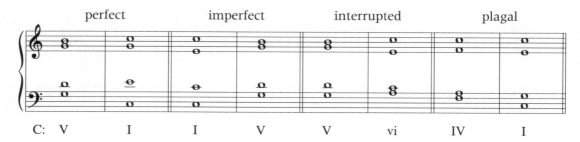

Perfect cadence

◆ The perfect cadence, or full close, is the 'full stop' of music and involves chord V moving to chord I.

◆ It creates an air of finality, helped by the melodic line, and will confirm the tonal centre or key in which it appears.

Here is an example of its use:

American and British national song

◆ The second chord of the cadence will usually be on a stronger beat than the first.

◆ In nearly all cases the chords appear in root position, with the bass moving from the dominant to the tonic. This strengthens the air of finality (but *see also* 'inverted cadences' on p. 53).

◆ The melodic line will normally move from the leading note to the tonic (*a*) or from the super-tonic to the tonic (*b*):

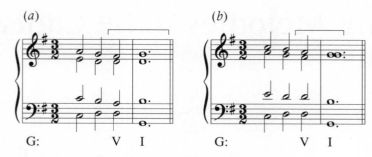

G: V   I   G: V   I

◆ The *tierce de Picardie*

In music written in a minor key you will often find a major chord, known as a *tierce de Picardie,* at the final cadence; invariably this occurs at a plagal cadence as well. (This custom derives from Renaissance harmonic practice, where to conclude on a minor chord was considered weak. The final cadence was either major, or the 3rd was omitted altogether.)

Exercise 30 Complete the following perfect cadences, using root position chords. Remember to check your work for consecutives! Put the two outer parts (soprano and bass) in place first, and then complete the harmony by adding tenor and alto parts.

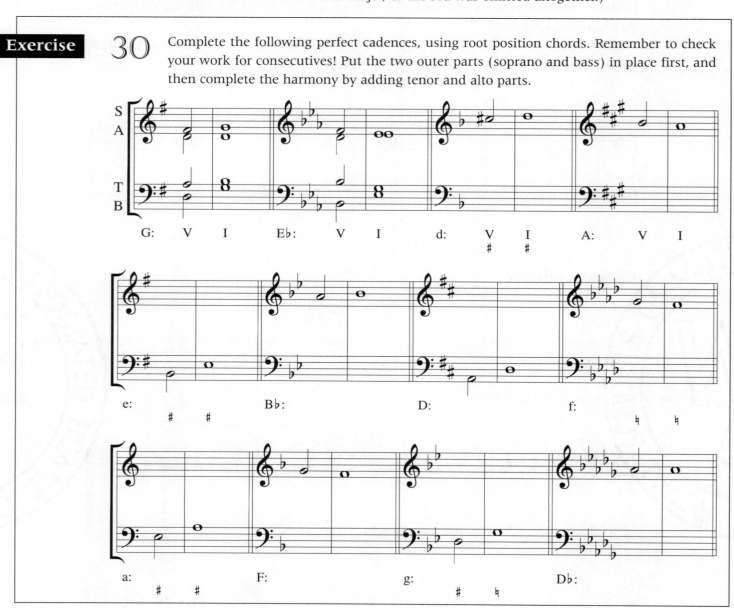

Imperfect cadence

◆ The imperfect cadence, or half close, is a temporary resting place in the melody, pausing on chord V. The imperfect cadence sounds less final than the perfect cadence.

◆ Several chords may precede V, including I, ii, IV and vi, and their first inversions.

◆ A succeeding phrase will normally return the music to the tonic chord with a perfect cadence.

Scottish Psalter (1635)

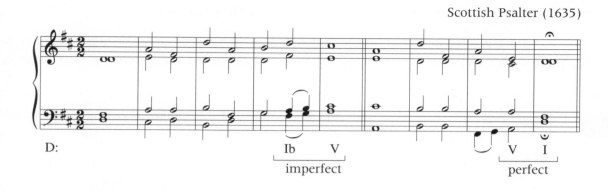

D: Ib   V   V   I
                                      imperfect   perfect

Exercise 31 Complete the following imperfect cadential progressions, first adding soprano or bass parts as appropriate and then completing the tenor and alto parts. Remember to check for consecutives and to sharpen the leading note in chord V in a minor key.

G: iib V   F: IV V   e: i v   C: vi V
   6   #

b: ii°b V   E: IV V   g: ib V   D♭: IVb V
   6   #   6   #   6

E♭: ii V   d: ii°b V   c: i V   A♭: IV V
              6   #   ♮

◆ Very occasionally, a sense of half close can come with a phrase that ends on a chord other than V. The first phrase of 'Auld Lang Syne', which ends on chord IV, is a good example:

'Auld Lang Syne'

G: I   IV

Perfect and imperfect cadences – some exercises

As we have seen, imperfect and perfect cadences often occur in succeeding melodic phrases. The music rests temporarily on an imperfect cadence, then more finally with a perfect cadence.

Exercise 32 Identify the perfect and imperfect cadences in the following extracts, taken from carols. Name the bracketed cadence and label the cadential chords involved.

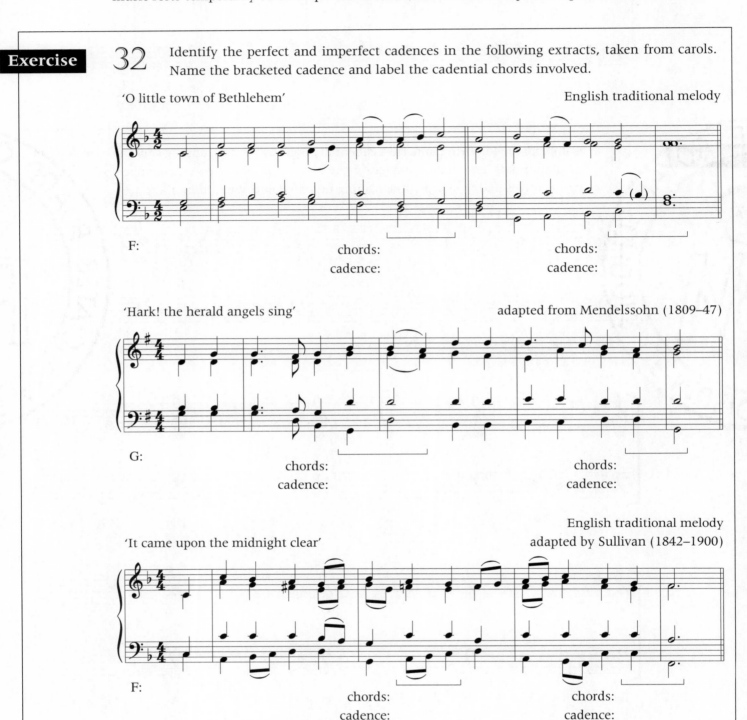

Short cadential phrases

We have looked at four-part primary chords in root position and seen their use in the important cadential progressions in tonal music. We have also noted a few 'rules' which tonal composers observed in their music, notably the 'consecutive rule'.

Below are some short cadential phrases for you to complete in four parts, with some guidelines for an appropriate working method.

Root position chords only

1 Take time to hum the melody line in your head. Use a keyboard to help you at this stage if you find it difficult.
2 Work out the key of the passage, then write out and label the triads of that key.
3 Label the chords of the progression, then write in the bass line and check for consecutives with the soprano part.
4 Now fill in the tenor and alto parts using only notes taken from the chosen triads.
5 Check for consecutives in the inner parts as you go.

Exercise 33 Using the method outlined above, complete the cadential phrases below. Remember to sharpen the leading note in minor keys.

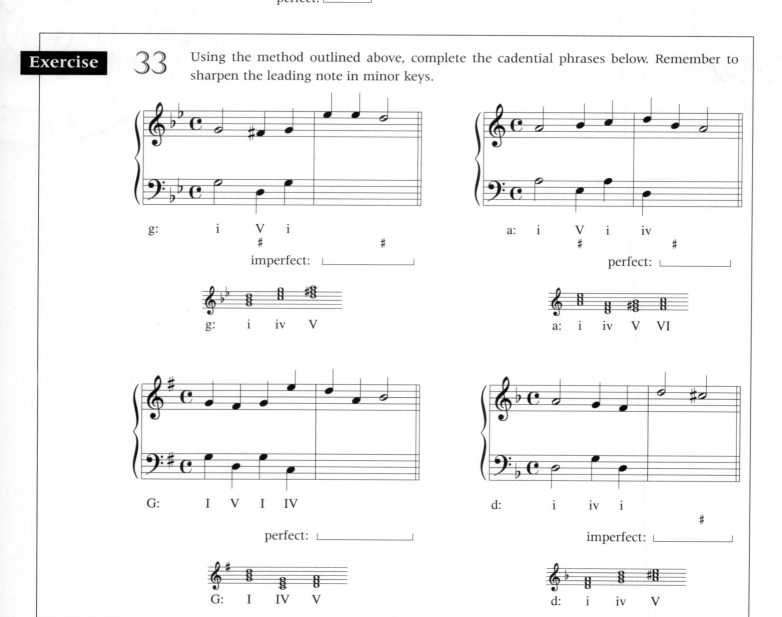

Cadences with chord inversions

In the following passages you will see how first inversion chords add variety to the harmonization. At a cadence, however, they do not sound as strong as root position chords.

The following example shows the same melodic phrase harmonized
- with root position chords at (a), and
- with a mix of root position and first inversion chords at (b).

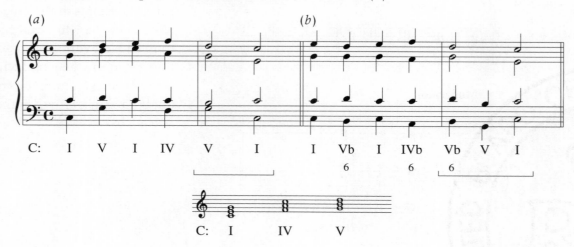

| C: | I | V | I | IV | V | I | | I | Vb | I | IVb | Vb | V | I |

Exercises 34   Identify and label
(a) the primary root position chords, and
(b) the root position and first inversion chords, identified by the figure 6.

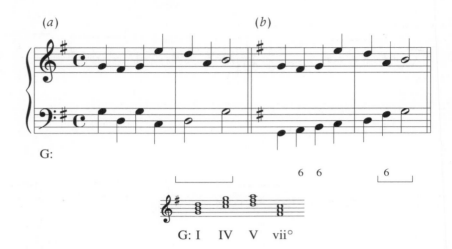

35 Now complete the harmonization in four parts. Check for consecutives.

36 Play both versions, noting the effect of the first inversion chords.

Traditional melodies

In the short cadential phrases above, each note was harmonized separately. But music does not always work this way. Look at the traditional melodies below and note the following:

◆ The **harmonic rhythm**, or rate of chord change, in these pieces is often quite slow: every two beats, every bar or every two bars, for example. This is in contrast to chorales and hymns, where the chord often changes on every beat.

◆ The harmonic rhythm often accelerates as the music approaches a cadence.

◆ These melodies, with their balancing phrases, are often harmonized using only tonic and dominant chords, with ii and IV appearing occasionally.

◆ There are several subsidiary or **decorating** notes in the melody lines, which may or may not belong to the harmony underneath. These are circled in the melodies below:

Exercises

37 Sing through the melodies, and mark the cadences with brackets. Label the cadences as perfect or imperfect and add a suitable bass line for them.

38 Identify and label the chords for each tune and add a simple bass line using long notes.

Melodic decoration†

We noted that the traditional melodies that you have just considered are elaborated with extra notes. These are present in most music, and are of several different kinds.

- (*a*) **Auxiliary harmony notes**, as their name suggests, are **consonant** or part of the chord suggested by the melody line.
- (*b*) **Passing notes** 'fill in' gaps between two harmony notes, smoothing out the melody with stepwise movement.
- (*c*) **Auxiliary notes** lie a tone or semitone above or below the harmony note. An auxiliary note ornaments the harmony note by simply alternating with it.

These types are usually found on weaker beats or half-beats of the bar.

'This old man'

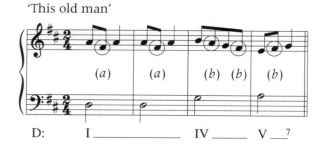

'Goosey, goosey gander'

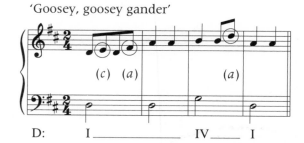

- (*d*) **Accented passing** and (*e*) **accented auxiliary notes** are related to (*b*) and (*c*), but they fall on the stronger beats and usually create a dissonance with the bass that needs to be resolved. The dissonant intervals they form against the bass will be 2nds, 4ths, 7ths or 9ths. They belong to the **appoggiatura** family of 'leaning' notes, and add to the harmonic effect as well as decorating the **melodic** line.
- (*f*) **Appoggiaturas** are accented dissonant decorations, approached by leap and 'resolved' by moving down or up by step. The dissonance created will invariably add expression and tension to the musical phrase.

'Lavender's blue'

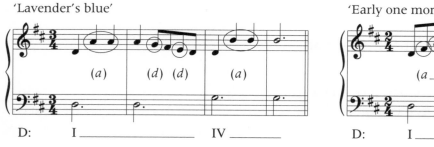

'Early one morning'

'Polly wolly doodle'

† This area is covered in more detail in Chapter 14.

In the following exercise you will see that it is possible to harmonize a phrase in more than one way. The second example in each case uses fewer chords and more melodic decorations.

Exercise 39   Identify the ringed notes as **auxiliary harmony** notes (h.),
                    auxiliary or **accented auxiliary** notes (aux. or a.aux.),
                    passing or **accented passing** notes (p.n. or a.p.n.), or
                    appoggiaturas (app.).

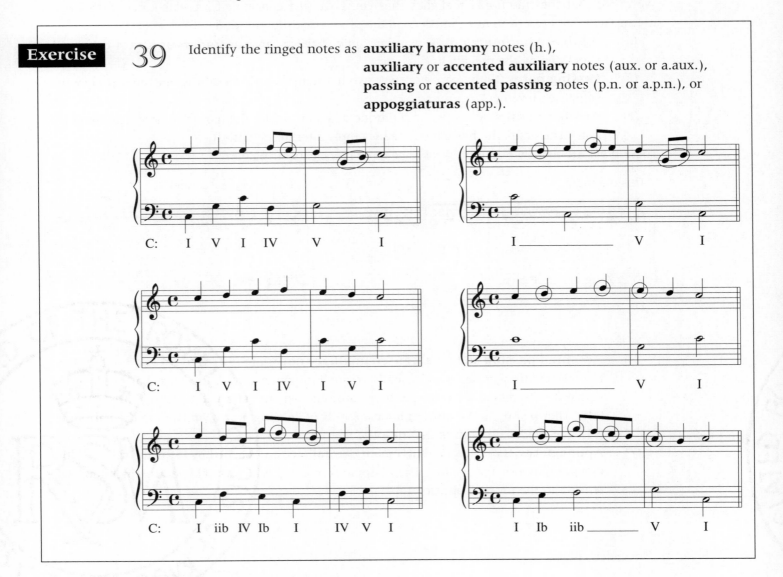

Interrupted and plagal cadences

Of lesser importance, because they occur infrequently compared with the perfect and imperfect cadences, are the interrupted and plagal cadences.

◆ The **interrupted cadence** is often a musical surprise. Instead of moving from chord V to chord I as the ear expects, the perfect cadence is 'interrupted' and moves to another chord, frequently vi, for example:

Bach: 'Sleepers wake', from Cantata 140 (1731)

◆ After the interruption, the phrase will normally be extended and lead to a perfect cadence.

◆ Note that in a minor key, it becomes necessary to double the major 3rd of chord VI, to avoid awkward part-writing. The 3rd of chord V would have to move through an augmented or diminished interval to either the root or 5th of chord VI (or there would be consecutive 5ths between the parts if the 5th of V moved to the 5th of VI).

g: V   VI

◆ In an interrupted cadence, chord V can move to other, more colourful chords. ♭VI, for instance, often follows, as in this example by Rossini. Other, even more exotic chords can follow, such as #iv^d7 (*see* Chapter 6, p. 84):

Allegro   Rossini: Overture, *The Silken Ladder* (1812)

C:

Tutti

V   ♭VI

C: V   ♭VI

◆ In a **plagal cadence**, the final chord I is preceded by IV, rather than V. In Renaissance sacred music it is found frequently at the ends of motets and other pieces, often on the word 'Amen' (*see* the example from the Scottish Psalter on p. 26). Mozart followed this tradition in the final bars of the 'Lacrymosa' and the 'Hostias' in his *Requiem* (1791).

Mozart: 'Lacrymosa', from *Requiem* (1791)

[re-] - - qui – em!   A – – men!

d: V   i   i♭7 I♭7_____ iv ivc ivb iv   I
                                        tierce de Picardie

◆ In the tonal period the plagal cadence was normally preceded by a V–I progression. The plagal ending simply confirmed the tonic key and often occurred at the very end of an extended cadential passage, where the home key had already been well established. The closing bars of Wagner's music dramas *Tristan and Isolde* and *The Ring of the Nibelung* illustrate this point.

Here is a shorter characteristic example!

Beethoven: 'Marcia funèbre', from Symphony No. 3 in E♭, 'Eroica' (1803)

(Adagio assai)

c: V⁷ i   iv i
                                          perfect   plagal

c: i iv V

Exercise 40 Complete the following cadences for SATB, marking the cadence as 'interrupted' or 'plagal' once you have completed it. Label the chords where necessary.

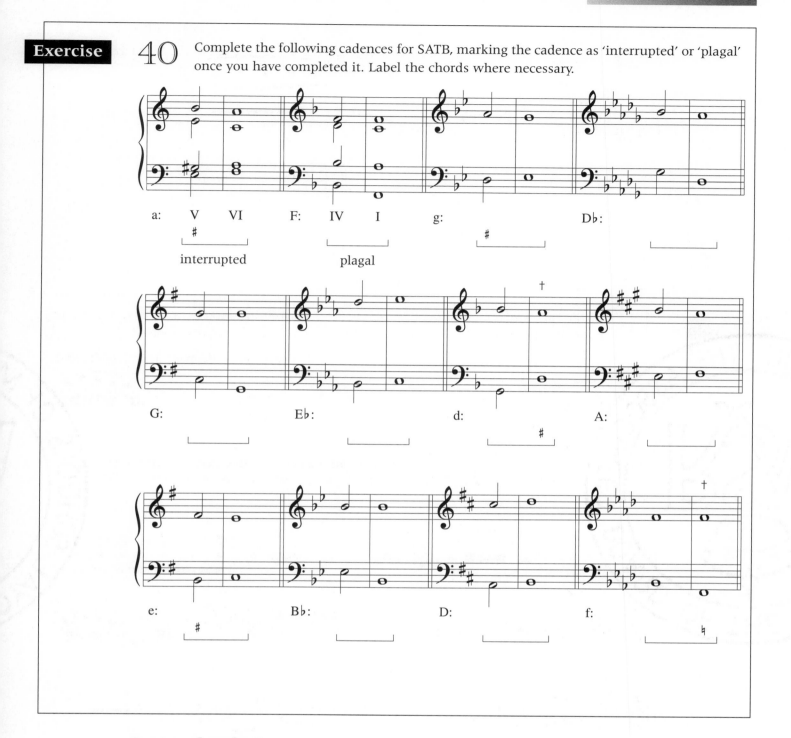

Inverted cadences

As we have seen, with the exception of the first chord of the imperfect cadence, the two chords of most cadential progressions are found in root position. There are exceptions, however, called **inverted cadences**. When one of the chords in a perfect, interrupted or plagal cadence is not in root position, or when the final chord of an interrupted or imperfect cadence is not in root position, then the cadence is inverted:

† Plagal cadences in a minor key normally feature a *tierce de Picardie*.

R143

Bach: Chorale

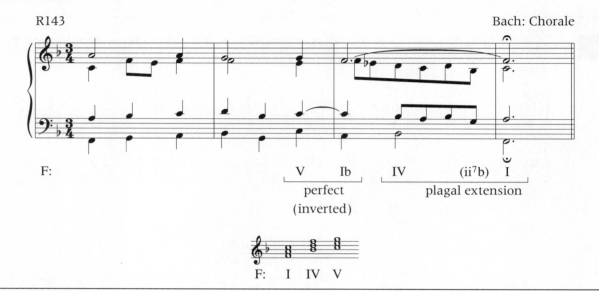

F:

V   Ib   IV   (ii⁷b)   I

perfect   plagal extension
(inverted)

F: I   IV   V

Exercise   **41**   In the following extracts identify the cadences marked in brackets as perfect, imperfect, interrupted or plagal. Play through the extracts and label the chords involved.

Mozart: Fantasia in C minor, K475 (1785)

(Adagio)

Mozart: Piano Sonata in A minor, K310 (1778)

Presto

a:

Beethoven: Piano Sonata in D minor, Op. 31 No. 2 (1802)

Allegretto

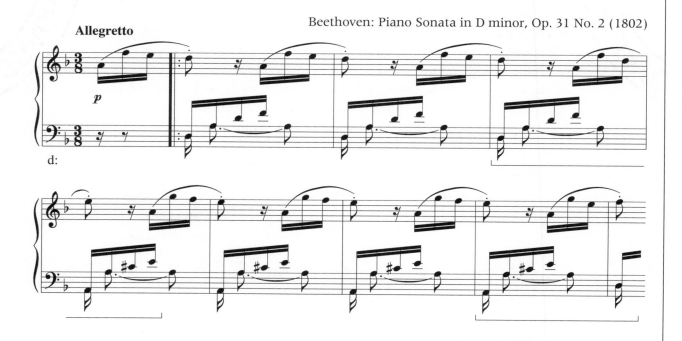

d:

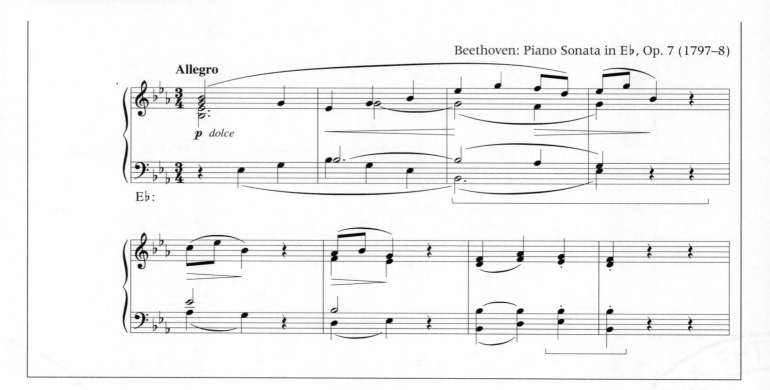

Beethoven: Piano Sonata in E♭, Op. 7 (1797–8)

Decoration at the cadence – the suspension†

We have seen that individual lines in a musical texture may often be decorated with, for example, auxiliary harmony notes, passing or auxiliary notes.

◆ In tonal music cadence points were traditionally decorated with notes **dissonant** with the bass, especially **suspensions**.

◆ These dissonances (2nds, 4ths, 7ths and 9ths) are always **prepared**, which means that the notes are sounded first as **consonances** in the previous chord, on a relatively weak beat, and held over, or 'suspended', on to a stronger beat.

◆ The suspension is then **resolved** downwards or, more rarely, upwards, by step on to a consonant harmony note. The resolution occurs on a beat weaker than the suspension.

◆ At the perfect cadence the '4–3' suspension is common:

R233   Bach: Chorale

† For a fuller discussion of the suspension *see* Chapter 14, p. 217.

◆ Notice that Bach drops his leading note to the 5th of the chord, rather than raising it to the tonic. This movement in an inside part is very common and results in a complete chord.

◆ In Baroque music, the **imperfect cadence** often features a '7–6' suspension:

Corelli: Concerto Grosso, Op. 6 No. 8 (pub. 1714)

◆ It is important to remember, then, that the suspension progression moves through three stages:
1 it is **prepared** as a **consonance** on a weak beat;
2 it **sounds** as a **dissonance** on a stronger beat, and
3 it **resolves** as a **consonance** on a subsequent weaker beat.

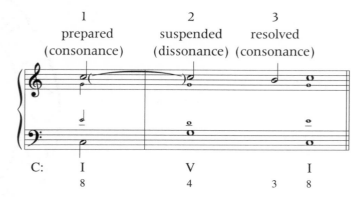

◆ The suspension, as its name implies, is usually tied. However, you will find many examples where the dissonant note is articulated.
◆ Suspensions are comparatively rare in the bass line (*see* Chapter 14).
◆ In the 4–3 suspension, the 3rd is rarely sounded **with** the dissonance, the 4th, since the effect is poor, and in the following example leads to consecutive octaves.

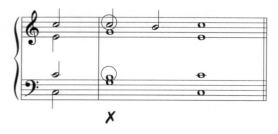

Exercise 42   Complete these cadential formulas which contain suspensions for SATB. The suspensions may occur in any part above the bass; most here are in the given soprano part.

◆ Always count the dissonance up from the bass, and **prepare**, **sound** and **resolve** the suspension in the **same** part.

The following cadential phrases are taken from Bach chorales:

1   write out the triads used in each extract;
2   label the harmony from the figured bass;
3   complete the extract for SATB;
4   check for consecutives.

Bach: Chorales
from '69 Chorale Melodies with Figured Bass'

Harmonizing melodies

The ability to harmonize a melody is a useful skill for practical musicians to develop and will reflect their awareness of different musical styles and techniques of composition. The choice of harmony will depend on the **character** of the given melody. For example, basic chords may suit a folk or popular song, changing perhaps every bar. A more sophisticated melody, by a composer like Liszt or Mahler for example, will suggest more elaborate, coloured harmony, and the melodies themselves may be decorated with chromatic notes and dissonances.

Your harmonizations should use the chords and progressions studied in this chapter.

Exercise 43 The following melodies include chords I, V and IV, with their first inversions.

1   Sing or play through the melody.

2   Write out the triads of the key.

3   First, mark the cadence points; it may help if you add phrase marks to the melody. Label the cadence chords.

4   Decide on the harmonic rhythm, that is, how often in the bar or phrase the harmony seems to change. This is normally on a strong beat, but there may be more chord changes at the approach to a cadence.

5   Choose all the other chords suggested by the melody line; there may be several possible harmonizations.

6   Add a bass line and check for consecutives with the melody.

7   Since some of the melodies may be familiar, you may be able to 'hear' a possible harmonization and therefore detect whether any chords you have selected sound out of place. Check your harmonization at the keyboard, filling in the chords and experimenting with different keyboard textures and chords if you are able.

Barnyard song

Folk-song from Kentucky, USA

'Dixie'

Southern army song of the American Civil War

'Will ye go, Lassie, go?'

Old Scottish ballad

Extending the Triad – the Dominant Family

CHAPTER 6

The addition of 7ths

◆ Triads can be extended by adding 3rds to make 7ths (and also 9ths, 11ths and 13ths) from the root. The extended chords are indicated by placing a small raised 7 (9, 11 or 13) after the numeral, e.g. I^7 or V^{11}.

◆ Like triads, these chords will vary in sound (major or minor, augmented or diminished) depending on the key. (For more about 9ths, 11ths and 13ths, *see* Chapter 15.)

Sing or play these examples:

$$I^7 \qquad ii^7 \qquad iii^7 \qquad IV^7 \qquad V^7 \qquad vi^7 \qquad vii^{\circ 7}$$

◆ The commonest extended chords are formed on chord V, but they can be heard used on any triad. A V^7 chord is called a **dominant 7th**.

◆ By adding a 7th, a further inversion is possible: the **third inversion** (d: for example, V^7d). In the third inversion the bass or lowest note is the 7th.

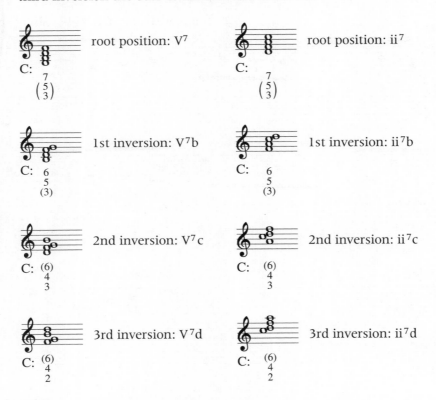

◆ Look at the figuring of the above inversions. In practice, the numbers shown in brackets were usually omitted, unless they needed alteration, e.g. 6♯.
$$\begin{smallmatrix}4\\3\end{smallmatrix}$$

◆ To determine the root of an inverted 7th chord, rearrange the notes so that they are stacked in 3rds; the lowest note is the root:

d: V⁷c

The root of this chord is A, so the chord on the left is in second inversion.

◆ Adding a 7th to a chord creates a sense of forward movement because of the tension it produces. The 7th note feels as though it should fall, and the usual movement of the bass note is to rise a 4th or fall a 5th.

C: vi⁷ - ii   ii⁷ - V   V⁷ - I

The forward movement created by this progression of 7th chords is very strong and it was used in music throughout the tonal period, becoming more common in music of the late eighteenth and nineteenth centuries. You will probably have noticed these 'chains' of 7th chords in music by Vivaldi, where the strong bass line adds to the satisfying nature of the progression. Here is a well-known example for you to play and enjoy!

Vivaldi: 'Winter' from *The Seasons*, Op. 8 No. 4 (pub. 1730)

We will look in more detail at this important progression in Chapter 9.

Exercises

44 Identify, label and figure these chords which contain 7ths. Some of the 7ths are in first inversion ($\frac{6}{5}$).

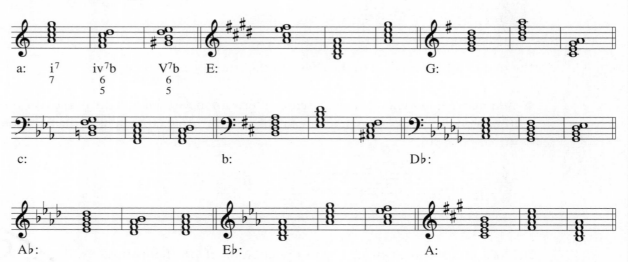

45 Write triads with the addition of a 7th as indicated, adding the figuring to each. Some of the triads are in first inversion.

The dominant 7th chord

◆ The dominant 7th chord, chord V with a 7th added to it, is one of the most important chords in tonal music as it leads strongly to the tonic chord, and so is often used at significant cadence points. It plays an important part in establishing new keys in **modulation** (*see* Chapter 12).

◆ Here is the dominant 7th chord in root position and its three inversions in the key of D major:

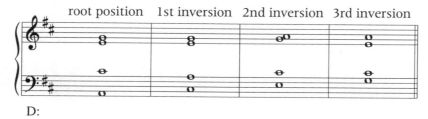

It is important to practise identifying and writing the chord in all its inversions and in various keys.

Exercises

46   Identify, label and figure the following dominant 7th chords.

47   Write dominant 7th chords as indicated, adding the figuring.

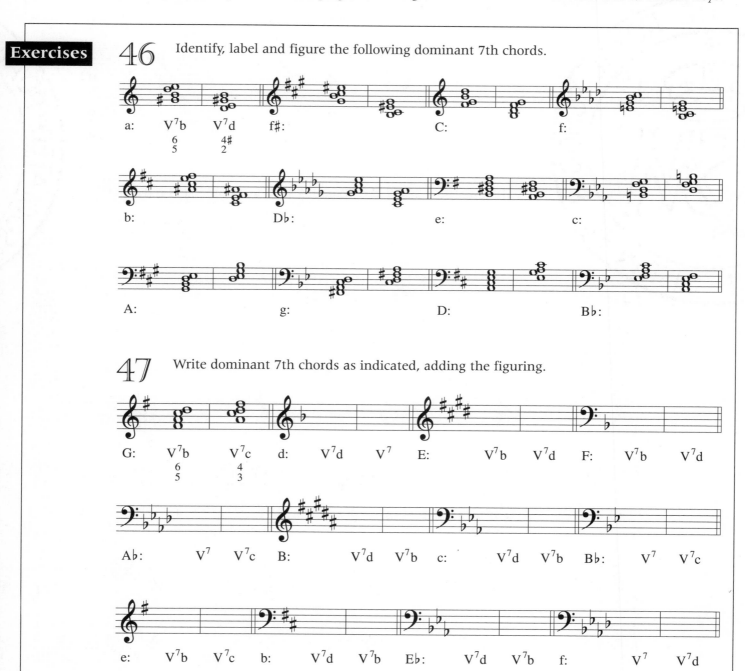

48   Label and figure these dominant 7th chords in various inversions and identify the keys.

f: V⁷b   B♭:   V⁷d
            6   4
            5   2

49   Write out and figure these inverted dominant 7th chords in the keys indicated.

B♭:   V⁷b   d: V⁷d   C: V⁷c   e: V⁷b
             6   4#
             5   2

A: V⁷d   E♭:   V⁷c   B: V⁷b   f: V⁷d   D: V⁷c

c#:   V⁷b   f: V⁷b   G: V⁷c   c: V⁷d   A♭:   V⁷b

The dominant 7th chord and its resolution

Early harmony arose out of vocal music, where the movement or line of each voice was the main consideration; the combination of lines resulted in the harmony. In rounds, canons and fugues, for example, the part-writing had priority; in other music, there was a distinction between a clear melody and an accompaniment, where the part-writing seemed less important. However, we shall see that much harmony is the result of individual lines which are subject to certain strong attractions, especially the melody and bass lines.

The dominant 7th leads to and strongly asserts the tonic because of various 'magnetic' pulls within the chord itself. The notes of the diminished triad above the bass note are 'unstable' and therefore require resolution. When the dominant bass note is added, the need for resolution is even more compelling.

In the progression V⁷–I:

- the key's leading note needs to rise;
- the chord's 7th needs to fall;
- the supertonic often falls;
- the dominant in the bass needs to move to its fundamental, the tonic.

Here are examples of each inversion of V⁷, together with their resolutions.

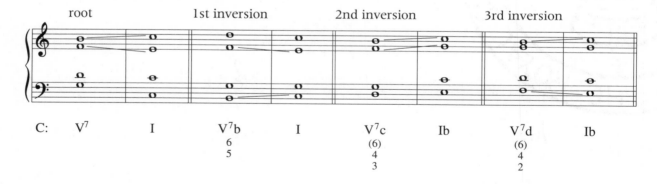

In the interests of part-writing, note the following:

◆ from a V⁷ chord in root position, three of the notes will resolve to the tonic in chord I;

◆ in the resolution of V⁷c–Ib, the 7th will often rise, probably because in that inversion the 7th does not form a dissonance with the bass, so the downward pull to resolve is not as strong;

◆ when the 7th of V⁷ is in the bass (V⁷d), it will normally resolve downwards, forming chord Ib.

Exercise 50 Write out, figure and resolve these dominant 7ths in the keys indicated. Remember to check for consecutives.

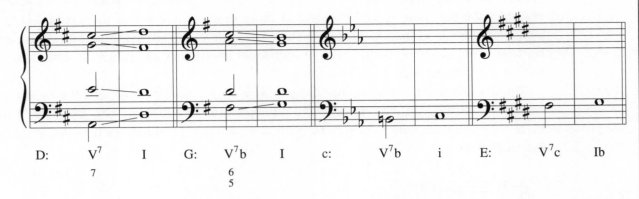

D: V⁷   I   G: V⁷b   I   c: V⁷b   i   E: V⁷c   Ib

Bb: V⁷d   Ib   A: V⁷b   I   C: V⁷c   I   d: V⁷d   ib

b: V⁷b   i   Db: V⁷   I   D: V⁷d   Ib   c: V⁷b   i

a: V⁷c   ib   F: V⁷b   I   Eb: V⁷   I   g: V⁷d   ib

e: V⁷   I   f: V⁷b   i   d: V⁷c   ib   c#:   V⁷b   i

◆ V[7]–I progressions will frequently dominate the harmony of a musical phrase, not just at the cadence. It is plain that this most basic of progressions can be found in a wide range of musical literature.

Schubert: Four Impromptus, Op. 90 No. 2 (1827)

Exercise 51 Play or listen to each of the following extracts, noting the sound and effect of the dominant 7th chord in root position and various inversions at the places marked with an asterisk. Label the positions and inversions as V⁷, V⁷b, etc.

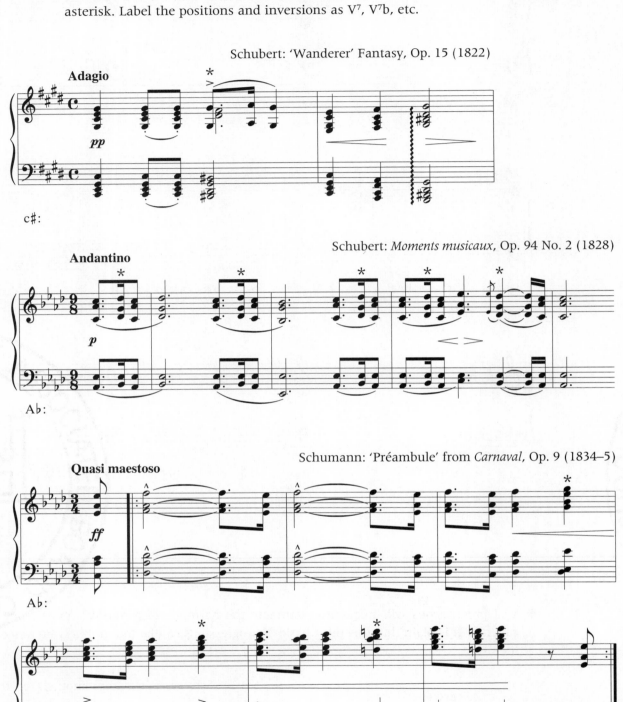

Schubert: 'Wanderer' Fantasy, Op. 15 (1822)

Schubert: *Moments musicaux*, Op. 94 No. 2 (1828)

Schumann: 'Préambule' from *Carnaval*, Op. 9 (1834–5)

Tchaikovsky: Symphony No. 6 in B minor, Op. 74, 'Pathétique' (1893)

Adagio lamentoso

b:

◆ Because the dominant 7th chord is so powerful in confirming the key, it is frequently used when a passage of music **modulates** (changes key).

◆ The dominant key itself is the strongest after the home key – one degree sharp away from the tonic – and therefore a move to the dominant is the most frequent modulation that we meet in tonal music. We shall look in more detail at this in Chapter 12, page 170.

Schumann: *Soldiers' March*, Op. 68 No. 2 (1832–48)

Munter und straff [Allegramente e risoluto]

G:

G: V⁷   I

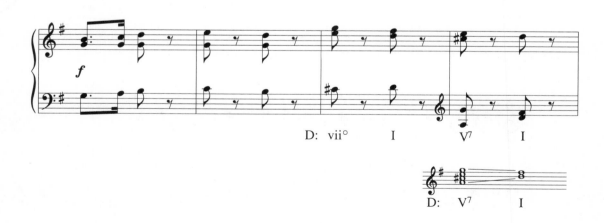

D: vii°   I   V⁷   I

D: V⁷   I

Exercises 52   Realize the figured bass in the following phrases for SATB:
1   label the chords;
2   fill in the alto and tenor parts;
3   check for consecutives.

53   Complete these phrases for SATB:
1   add the bass line and check for consecutive movement;
2   add the alto and tenor parts and check for consecutives.

54   Add a melody line and realize the figured bass for SATB:

1   label the chords;
2   add the soprano part. Sing through the melody and satisfy yourself that the line sounds natural and convincing;
3   check for consecutive movement between bass and soprano;
4   add the alto and tenor parts and check for consecutives.

Chord vii – the dominant family extended

viib

Notice that the upper three notes of the dominant 7th are the same as chord vii°. Chord vii° is sometimes used as an alternative to chord V⁷, although it lacks the strong root. It does contain the interval of the diminished 5th, which needs to resolve, and the leading note, which needs to rise to the tonic. The chord is part of the large dominant family.

The following points should be noted about chord vii°:
* its sound quality is of a diminished chord;
* it appears only rarely in root position – it is usually in first inversion (vii°b);
* it is best to double the bass note of vii°b, i.e. the 3rd of the chord, rather than the root, which is the leading note and is rarely doubled.

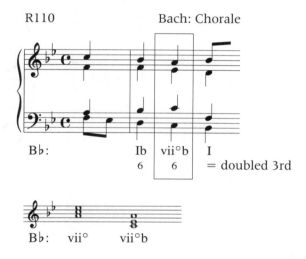

The passing vii°b or passing ⁶₃

◆ We have seen that vii°b–I does not make a very conclusive cadence, because it lacks the dominant note in the bass. It appears more frequently as the **passing vii°b** or **passing ⁶₃**. This is often used to harmonize scale passages in which the tonic chord moves between first inversion and root position chords, and less frequently between root position and first inversion chords (*see* Chapter 11):

Bach: Chorales

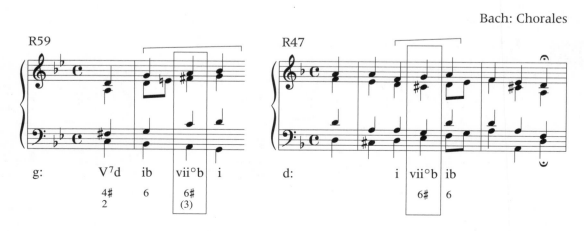

◆ This is a very similar progression to the passing $\frac{6}{4}$ (*see* Chapter 7, p. 98). Compare these two examples:

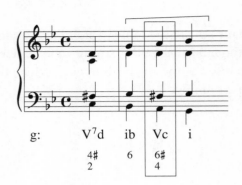

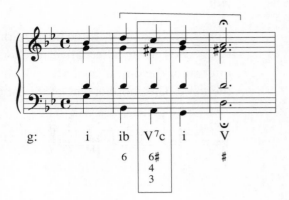

◆ The passing vii°b ($\frac{6}{3}$) is often decorated, either with a 7–6 suspension (*a*), or with an accented passing note (*b*) (*see* Chapter 5):

(*a*)

R140

(*b*)   Bach: Chorales

R120

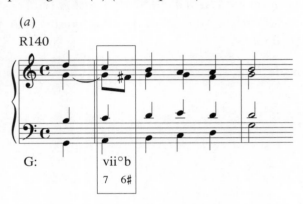

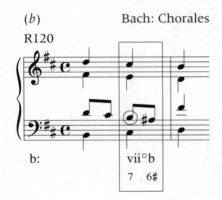

◆ The passing vii°b ($\frac{6}{3}$) may also arise from chord ii. In the following example, vii°b appears to be a passing note on the quaver beat:

R63   Bach: Chorale

Exercises   *55*   Label the chords in these examples.

R81

R74   Bach: Chorales

56 Complete these phrases, containing the passing vii°b ($^6_3$), in four parts. Add labelling and figuring where possible.

◆ Chord vii°b (♭VIIb) may also be heard in a progression of first inversion chords:

(Adagio)   Corelli: Trio Sonata, Op. 2 No. 4 (1685)

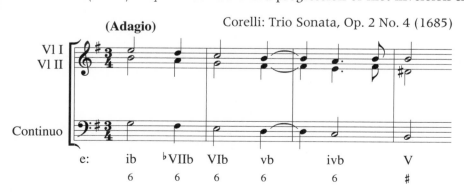

Exercise *57*   Label the chords in the following extracts.

Buxtehude: Cantata *Das neugeborne Kindelein* (?*c*.1680)

(d):

Gigue   Handel: Suite No. 9 in G minor (pub. 1733)

F:

Haydn: Piano Sonata in E♭, Hob XVI/49 (1789–90)

E♭:

Beethoven: Piano Concerto No. 4 in G, Op. 58 (1805–6)

G:

The diminished 7th

The **diminished 7th chord** creates one of the most characteristic and arresting sounds of the tonal era. It is often formed by adding a minor 3rd to vii° and, like any 7th chord, can appear in root position or one of three inversions. The extra 3rd creates the interval of a diminished 7th from the bass note.

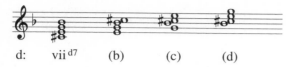

d: vii ᵈ⁷   (b)   (c)   (d)

◆ It is indicated by ᵈ⁷ after the chord numeral. The diminished 5th is implied in the diminished 7th and therefore the ° is omitted.

◆ Notice that each interval between the notes of the chord is a minor 3rd. Whatever the inversion, the chord always consists of stacks of **sounding** minor 3rds, so all the inversions have the same sound quality. It is only on paper, where the 'spelling' of the chord is apparent, that the true root can be found. The notation will indicate which of the notes are chromatic and which are part of the key, e.g. the minor 3rd sound is expressed as an augmented 2nd at the top of the chord in (b), indicating A minor.

c: vii ᵈ⁷   a: vii ᵈ⁷b

◆ The diminished 7th can in fact be built on any degree of the scale. All twelve semitones are found in three diminished 7ths, and the chord plays an important part in chromatic harmony and modulation (*see* Chapter 12, p. 170 for an example and the exercises on p. 174).

We shall examine some of the ways this chord is used in Chapter 13. Here now is some practice in writing and identifying the chord.

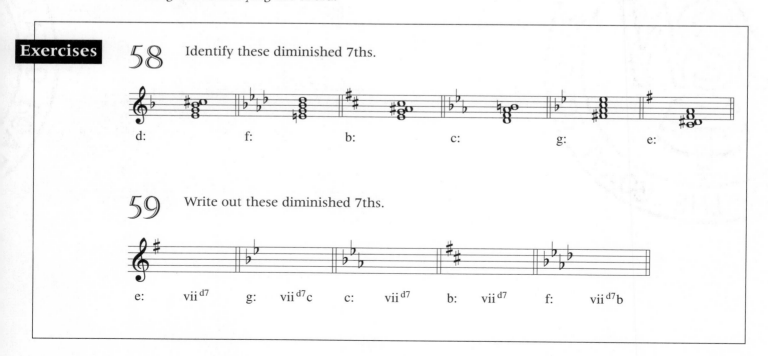

Exercises

58   Identify these diminished 7ths.

d: f: b: c: g: e:

59   Write out these diminished 7ths.

e: vii ᵈ⁷   g: vii ᵈ⁷c   c: vii ᵈ⁷   b: vii ᵈ⁷   f: vii ᵈ⁷b

Chord vii^{d7}

◆ Its principal use is as a substitute for V, when a 'darker' colouring is suggested.
◆ During the Baroque and Classical periods it was normally found in a minor key, though in the nineteenth century it became common in the major key as well.
◆ The diminished 7th is sometimes called the **rootless minor 9th**:

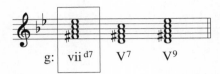

In the following example notice the difference the E♭ makes to the sound of the diminished 7th chord in (*a*) contrasted with the major sound of chord V⁷b in (*b*):

(*a*)   R297   Bach: Chorale   (*b*)

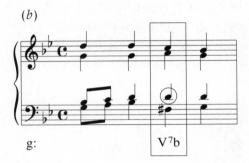

Exercises   60   Write vii^{d7} on one stave and resolve it on to i in the keys suggested. Notice in the first example how the notes of the diminished 7th chord resolve by step to the notes of the tonic chord. Use different inversions. Play through the examples in order to memorize the sound of this important chord.

61   Complete the vii^{d7} chords in the following chorale passages and then play them through.

Bach: Chorales

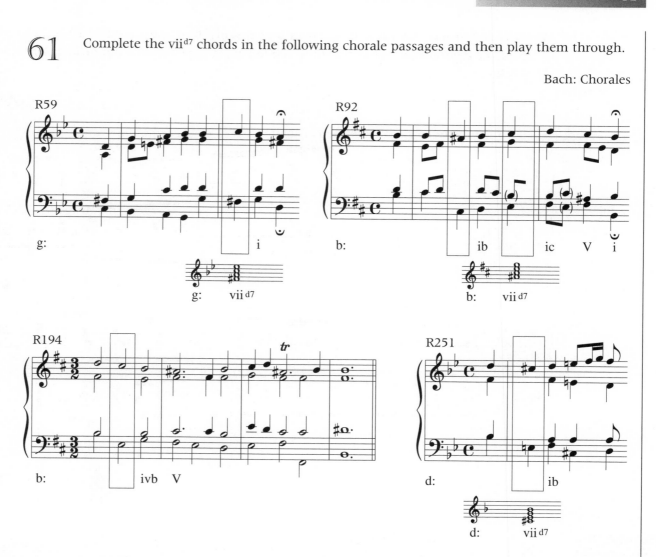

The diminished 7th chord is found in much descriptive music and is able to highlight all manner of dramatic and emotional situations, that is, to 'move the passions'.[†] Purcell uses it over a chromatic **ground bass** (a recurring bass-line pattern) in Dido's Lament, in the last part of his opera *Dido and Aeneas*.

Purcell: Dido's Lament from *Dido and Aeneas* (1689)

[†] The English music publisher Henry Playford commended Purcell as 'having a peculiar genius to express the Energy of English words whereby he moved the Passions in all his auditors'.

◆ Even in instrumental music, where words are **not** involved, the diminished 7th chord still carries the same emotional weight. In both of the following examples the diminished 7th chord marks the climax of the movement.

Bach: Prelude in B♭ minor, from *The Well-Tempered Clavier*, Bk 1 No. 22 (1722)

(Andante, largamente ma non adagio)

Beethoven: Piano Sonata in F minor, Op. 57 'Appassionata', 1st movt (1804)

◆ In the same sonata, Beethoven uses the diminished 7th to mark the transition to the third movement and for the dramatic outburst of its opening bars:

Beethoven: Piano Sonata in F minor, Op. 57 'Appassionata', 2nd/3rd movts (1804)

Chord $\sharp\text{iv}^{\text{d7}}$

Apart from the diminished 7th built on the leading note (vii^{d7}), the other diminished 7th often heard in eighteenth- and nineteenth-century harmony is an altered version of chord iv, i.e. $\sharp\text{iv}^{\text{d7}}$. As such it is vii^{d7} of the dominant and usually resolves on to that chord.

The notation is self-explanatory: $\sharp\text{iv}$ indicates that the root of iv has been sharpened (*a*); $\sharp\text{iv}^{\text{d7}}$ indicates that the chord over the $\sharp\text{iv}$ is a diminished 7th (*b*):

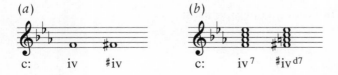

In the early nineteenth century Weber used it in his opera *Der Freischütz*. Played on tremolando strings, it evokes the spine-chilling presence of the devil Zamiel:

Weber: *Der Freischütz* (1817–21)

The familiar example below sums up the character of chord #iv^{d7}.

Exercises 62 Identify and label the chord marked with an asterisk in the following extract and circle any other diminished 7ths.

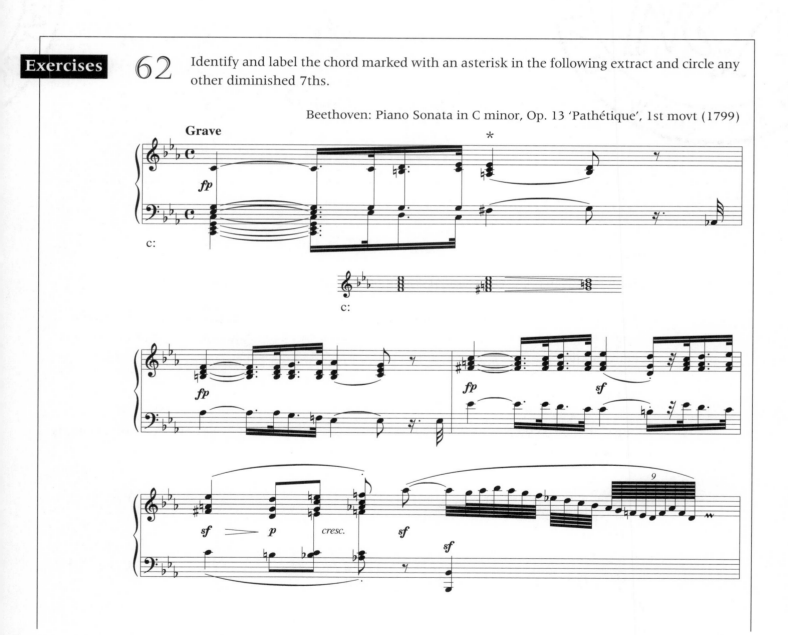

Beethoven: Piano Sonata in C minor, Op. 13 'Pathétique', 1st movt (1799)

63   Complete the ♯iv^{d7} chords in the following chorale phrases and play them through.

Bach: Chorales

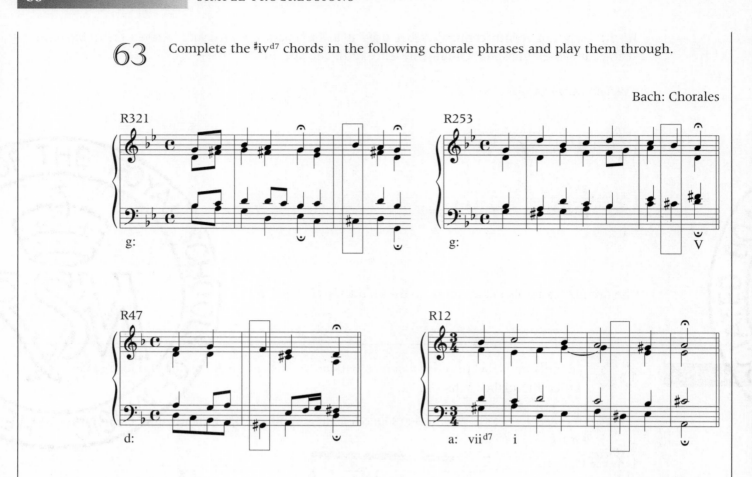

Chord iii (III)

Of all the triads in a key, chord iii (III) can most effectively play more than one role.

◆ Apart from its position in the progression of 5ths (*see* Chapter 9) between vii and vi, chord iii is found in both tonic and dominant families. It can act as a substitute for the tonic or the dominant chord.

1 As part of the tonic group

◆ Chord iii may be seen as a close relation or extension of I, since it is part of I⁷. Like other chords that are part of the tonic group it moves then to IV or ii.

Bach: Chorale

◆ We can hear it used as a substitute for I in late nineteenth-century French music, where its rather ambiguous nature is typical of the style.

Fauré: 'Pie Jesu', from *Requiem* (1893)

2 As part of the dominant group

◆ In first inversion chord iii has the dominant as the bass note, and so iiib can act as a substitute for the dominant chord.

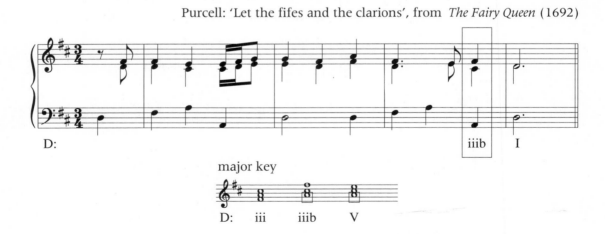

Purcell: 'Let the fifes and the clarions', from *The Fairy Queen* (1692)

◆ It is often used to harmonize the flattened leading note in a descending melodic minor scale (*see* Chapter 11, p. 153).

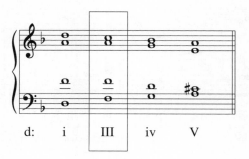

◆ The augmented triad III+b, found in the minor key, is a characteristic sound in the music of Purcell and also the English madrigalists, where it is often used for expressive purposes:

Weelkes: 'O care, thou wilt despatch me' (1600)

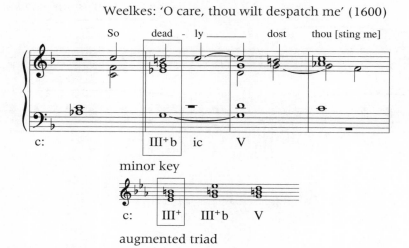

Exercises   **64**   Identify chords iii, iiib and III+b in the following extracts, noting the different sound quality of each chord.

Use the following extracts to help you to remember these sounds. You will notice that the sound of the augmented triad (III+b) is more often than not a result of movement in the part-writing decorating the dominant chord, as in the Mozart example below:

Dowland: 'In darkness let me dwell' (1610)

Purcell: 'If love's a sweet passion', from *The Fairy Queen* (1692)

g:

(Adagio)   Mozart: 'Introitus', from *Requiem* (1791)

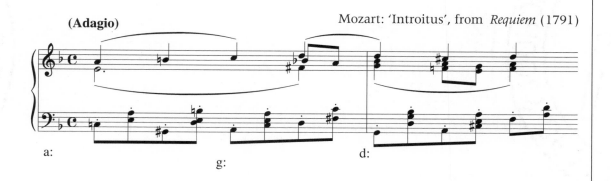

a: g: d:

R110   Bach: Chorale

f: c:

Andante   Shostakovich: Piano Concerto No. 2, Op. 102 (1957)

C:

65   Complete these passages for SATB which include versions of chord iii.

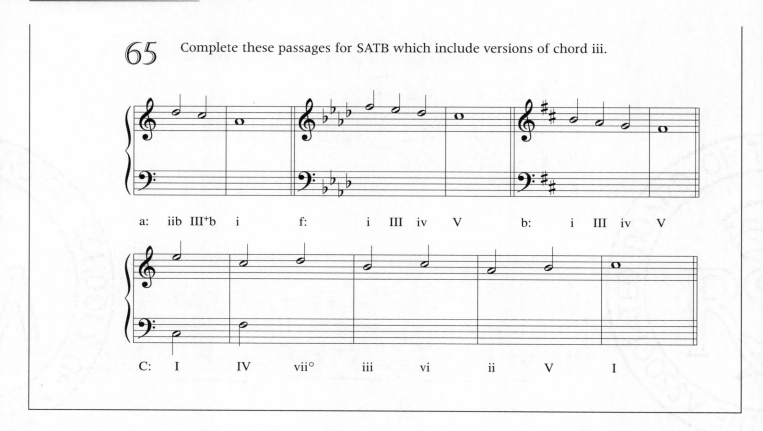

a: iib III⁺b i   f: i   III iv   V   b: i   III iv   V

C: I   IV   vii°   iii   vi   ii   V   I

Chord iii **can** suggest tonic or dominant harmony, but frequently it creates a nebulous, rather vague impression. For this reason it is not often found in strongly tonal music, for example that of Bach, Mozart or Beethoven.

The $\frac{6}{4}$ Progressions

Tonal composers generally used second inversion chords only in the following three contexts:

(*a*) as a decoration of V, on a strong beat: the **cadential** $\frac{6}{4}$ (Ic–V);

(*b*) as a **passing** chord, on a **weak** beat: Ib–Vc–I or IV–Ic–IVb;

(*c*) as an **auxiliary** $\frac{6}{4}$, on a weak or strong beat: I–IVc–I.

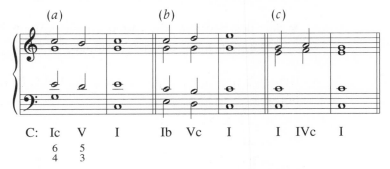

The common progressions or uses of the second inversion chord are given below, together with some examples and exercises, so that you can learn to recognize their sound.

The cadential $\frac{6}{4}$

◆ One of the most characteristic progressions in tonal music is the cadential $\frac{6}{4}$: Ic–V. It is a particular feature of the Classical style, where it may form an imperfect or interrupted cadence, or part of a perfect cadence.

Mozart: Piano Sonata in F, K280 (1774)

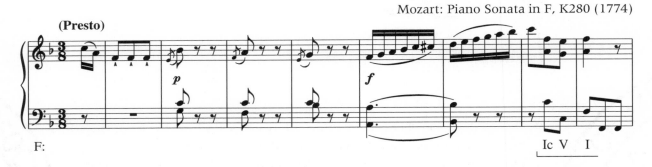

As you become familiar with the sound of the second inversion chord you will recognize that in tonal music it does not have the same 'stand alone' quality as root position and first inversion chords. There is a sense that the $\frac{6}{4}$ chord needs to progress or move in a certain way. This is because the notes that make up the $\frac{6}{4}$ chord are really ornaments – accented passing notes, appoggiaturas (leaning notes), or suspensions – which decorate the melodic line, and therefore resolve naturally downwards. Consider these two passages from Mozart piano sonatas:

Mozart: Piano Sonata in B♭, K281 (1774)

Without the decoration this passage would appear as:

◆ The decoration at the cadence creates the $^6_4$–$^5_3$ progression, the cadential $^6_4$. In this example the decoration notes are suspensions.

Here is a similar example of the cadential $^6_4$. In this case the decoration notes are accented passing notes.

Mozart: Piano Sonata in B♭, K282 (1774)

without decoration at the cadence:

◆ Second inversion chords contain the interval of a 4th from the bass. The 4th, like the 7th that we met in Chapter 6, is a dissonance that needs to resolve, usually by step downwards. The same tension is found in chords that contain 9ths or 2nds, which are also dissonances. This was discussed in Chapter 5 when looking at suspensions.

Here are some basic examples of the cadential $^6_4$:

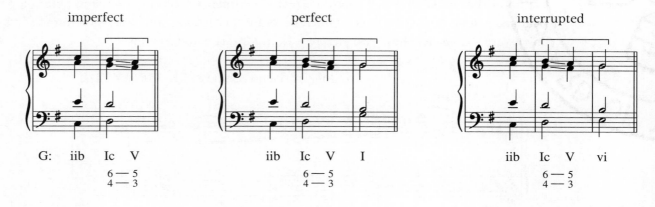

  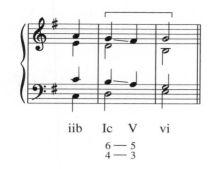

G: iib Ic V
6 — 5
4 — 3

iib Ic V I
6 — 5
4 — 3

iib Ic V vi
6 — 5
4 — 3

Note the following:
- the smooth melody lines, which are very common at cadences;
- the doubled bass note (the 5th of the chord);
- the resolution of the 6th to the 5th, 6–5, and the 4th to the 3rd, 4–3;
- the chord falling on a strong beat.

 Exercises 66 Complete in four parts these cadence patterns which use the $\frac{6}{4}$, using the labelling and figuring to help you.

D: IV IVc I iib Ic V e: ic V i ic V I
6 — 5 / 4 — 3 ... 6 ... 6 — 5 / 4 — 3 ... 6 — 5 / 4 — # ... 6 — 5 / 4 — # ... #

F: iib Ic V IV Ic V b: ic V i ic V i
6 ... 6 — 5 / 4 — 3 ... 6 — 5 / 4 — 3 ... 6 — 5 / 4 — # ... 6 — 5 / 4 — #

Bb: Ic V I Ic V I g: ic V i ic V I
6 — 5 / 4 — 3 ... 6 — 5 / 4 — 3 ... 6 — 5 / 4 — # ... 6 — 5 / 4 — # ... ♮

67   Label and complete the $^6_4$–$^5_3$ progressions in these cadences from chorales by Bach.

Bach: Chorales

† Modal key signature.

68 Label the asterisked chords and identify the cadences in the following extracts.

Handel: Suite No. 3 (pub. 1720)

Bach: French Suite No. 6 in E (*c.*1725)

Handel: Chaconne with Sixty-two Variations (Variation 4)

◆ In triple time, the ⁶₄ occasionally appears to fall on a weak beat, as in the next example. At a cadence, however, the accents of two three-beat bars are often grouped so that they fall into three sets of two beats, a rhythm known as **hemiola**. The ⁶₄ now comes on a strong beat. Sometimes the correct stresses are shown by adding brackets, as below. This so-called **cross-rhythm** moves the music strongly towards the cadence.

Handel: Air, HWV 467 (*c.*1720)

◆ The resolution of the $\frac{6}{4}$ to the $\frac{5}{3}$ is sometimes delayed by a note or a chord 'sandwiched' in between. This may involve a melodic decoration, such as the ***échappée*** note (*a*) (*see* Chapter 14, p. 208), or an appoggiatura (*b*) (*see* Chapter 5, p. 49):

Bach: Chorales

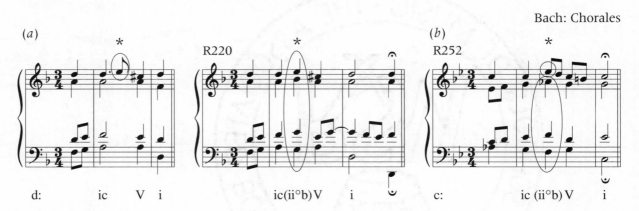

Exercise **69** Label the chords in these examples.

Bach: Chorales

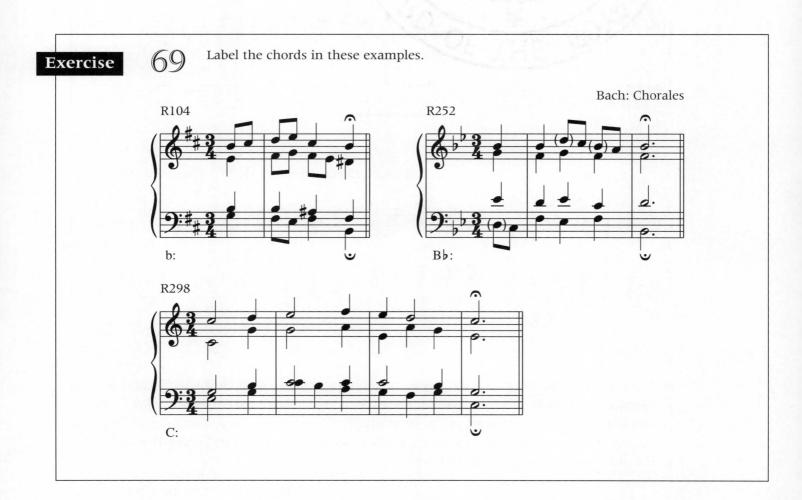

By the end of the eighteenth century, in the Classical period, the $\frac{6}{4}$ was fully established on the strong beat, and occurred very frequently at both perfect and imperfect cadences. The prevailing 'weak ending' phrase, matching the Italian language used in most opera, became universal in all forms of music.

Mozart: *The Marriage of Figaro*, Act IV (1786)

'O come, do not delay, my heart's dear treasure,
Come where fond love is calling thee to pleasure,...'

Exercise **70** Play or listen to the following extracts from Mozart sonatas. Identify the cadences and label the chords involved.

Mozart: Piano Sonata in B♭, K333 (1778)

Mozart: Piano Sonata in D, K311 (1777)

Mozart: Piano Sonata in C, K309 (1777)

The passing $^6_4$

◆ In this progression the second inversion chord appears in a smooth scale movement on a weak beat. Characteristic progressions are I–Vc(^{7})–Ib or IV–Ic–IVb:

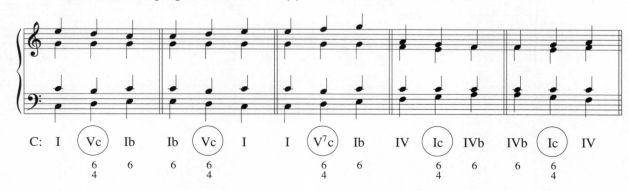

Exercise

71   Identify and label the asterisked chords in the following extracts.

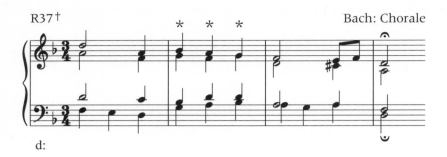

d:

C:

E♭:

72   Complete the following progressions of the passing $\frac{6}{4}$. Add the figuring.

D: a:

c: g:

† From '69 Chorale Melodies with Figured Bass' from G. C. Schemelli's *Gesangbuch* (published 1736).

The auxiliary $^6_4$

◆ In this progression the upper notes of the $^6_4$ chord behave like auxiliary notes (*see* Chapter 5, p. 49), moving away from and back to the original chord by step. The auxiliary $^6_4$ chord is usually IVc.

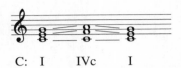

C: I   IVc   I

◆ You will often find IVc over a tonic pedal.

Exercises

73   Label the asterisked chords in the following extracts. Play the extracts and listen to the effect of the auxiliary $^6_4$.

74   The following extracts contain bracketed examples of the various uses we have so far examined of a ⁶₄ chord. Mark with an asterisk the ⁶₄ chords and identify them as cadential, passing or auxiliary.

Petzold: from *Little Notebook for Anna Magdalena Bach* (1725)

Menuet II

F:

Bach: Suite in E♭, BWV 819/3 (*c.*1722)

Sarabande

E♭:

Mozart: Piano Sonata in D, K311 (1777)

Andante con espressione

G:

Mozart: Piano Sonata in D, K576 (1789)

D:

75 Realize these passages for SATB voices. The $\frac{6}{4}$ chords appear as either cadential, passing or auxiliary $\frac{6}{4}$s. Check for consecutives, and remember to double the **bass** note of the $\frac{6}{4}$ chord.

The $^6_4$ and the cadenza

We have seen that the second inversion is an important cadential chord in tonal music. In the Baroque and Classical periods particularly, a $^6_4$ cadence was often elaborated by a cadenza or a flourishing phrase when it came at an important point in the piece. In the Baroque aria, for example, it became the custom for the singer to improvise a florid phrase on the $^6_4$ chord of the final vocal cadence:

Handel: *Messiah* (1742)

Similarly, in a Classical concerto from around 1740, where the score indicates a pause on chord Ic, the soloist would improvise a cadenza. The cadenza would then end with a trill on a root position dominant chord and a perfect cadence.

Mozart: Piano Concerto in A, K488 (1786)

Mozart's cadenza
Solo piano

Such a cadential trill on chord V⁷, preceded by Ic, was in fact a feature of Classical keyboard music in general:

Mozart: Piano Sonata in C, K545 (1788)

◆ You should restrict use of the $\frac{6}{4}$ chord to the three types we have met so far: the cadential, passing and auxiliary $\frac{6}{4}$. There is, however, one other context in which the $\frac{6}{4}$ chord regularly appears. Sometimes the bass line outlines the notes of a chord, forming root position, first and second inversions of the chord. The following three examples illustrate the point well.

American and British national song

G: I   Ib   Ic   I   V⁷   V⁷b   V⁷c   V⁷

Beethoven: Piano Sonata in A♭, Op. 110 (1821–2)

(Allegro molto)

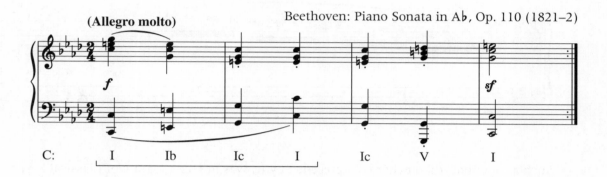

C: I   Ib   Ic   I   Ic   V   I

Schubert: *Erlkönig*, Op. 1 (1815)

Schnell (♩ = 152)

g: i   iv   ic   ib   i

◆ In the late Romantic period the $^6_4$ chord was used more freely. In the music of Richard Strauss and Edward Elgar it sometimes featured as the climactic chord of a phrase, to great effect. Such a moment is found in Elgar's oratorio *The Dream of Gerontius* (1900) on the words 'Praise to the holiest in the height':

Elgar: *The Dream of Gerontius* (1900)

Maestoso

C: Ic

Other Presentations of Harmony

CHAPTER 8

Although some textbooks and examinations might suggest otherwise, 'harmony' does not exist only as four-part writing. All tonal music will suggest or imply harmony, even if the texture does not make it obvious.

Single lines

The notes in a chord do not necessarily need to be sounded at the same time. Even a single line will imply harmony. Scales and arpeggio figurations can be translated as chord progressions.

Much of J. S. Bach's music can be 'untangled' in this way. For example, the magnificent sonatas and partitas for unaccompanied violin and the suites for cello and for lute all contain elaborate writing. In the example below, most of the notes, including those on the strong beats, are harmony notes belonging to chord I (E, G♯, B). Other notes add decoration to the basic chord:

In this next example, from the first Cello Suite in G, more harmonies are implied.

Exercise *76*   Identify the harmony in the following extract and label the chords.

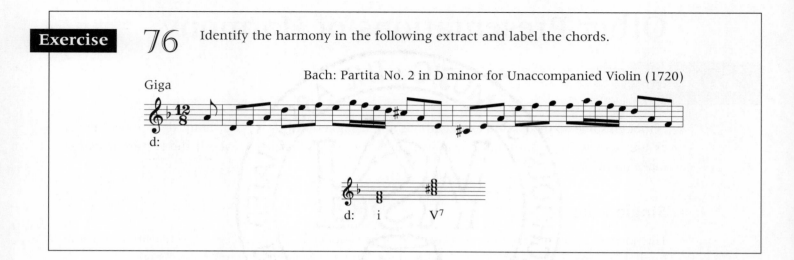

Bach: Partita No. 2 in D minor for Unaccompanied Violin (1720)

◆ Many Classical pieces begin with a musical 'call to attention' which establishes the tonic key. The notes of chord I, for instance, can be played in unison as a fanfare:

Haydn: Symphony No. 104 in D, 'London' (1795)

◆ Sometimes there is an answer on the dominant chord:

Mozart: Serenade in G, *Eine kleine Nachtmusik*, K525 (1787)

Exercise *77*   Label the chords implied in these unison passages.

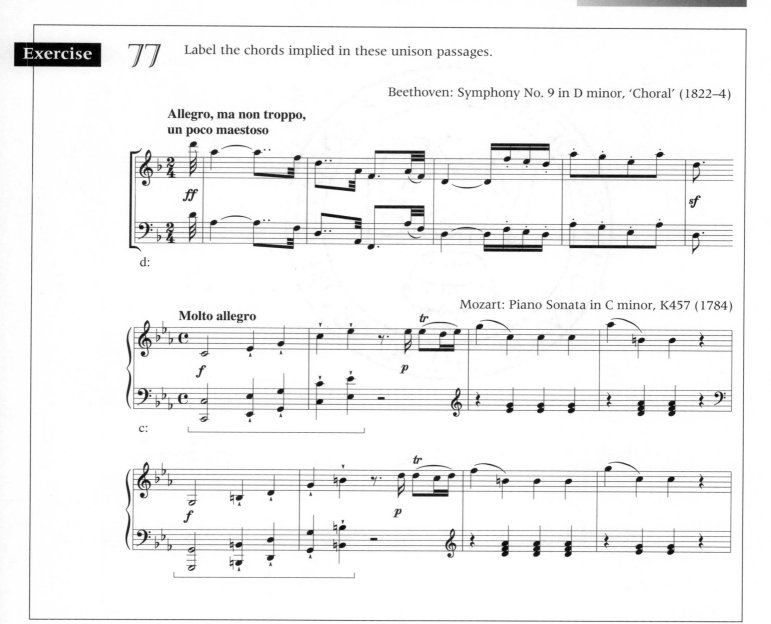

Beethoven: Symphony No. 9 in D minor, 'Choral' (1822–4)

Mozart: Piano Sonata in C minor, K457 (1784)

Two parts

Even two-part writing can suggest harmony.

Out of context

D:

could suggest several chords, including:

D: ii   viiºb   Vc

but in a tonal progression the ear will 'fill in' the missing notes in a two-part texture.

Jeremiah Clarke: *The Prince of Denmark's March* (c.1674–1707)

Much Baroque keyboard music is written in two parts. Purcell, Couperin, Handel, Bach and Scarlatti, among others, regarded two-part textures as perfectly adequate to their needs.

Extra harmony notes give weight, especially at cadences.

Petzold: from *Little Notebook for Anna Magdalena Bach* (1725)

In early Classical and Rococo styles the harmonies were often broken up into repeated figurations, the so-called **Alberti bass**. These appear in both fast and slow tempi but are particularly effective in lyrical passages.

Mozart: Piano Sonata in D, K284, 3rd movt (Variation 11) (1775)

The following exercises will help you to work out harmonic progressions from two-line textures by reducing the lines to the chords implied.

Exercise 78 On the small stave beneath the music, condense the notes of the texture into the chords implied, working from the bass or lowest part. Then identify which chords are being used and label them. The notes in brackets are dissonant (that is, they create 2nds, 4ths or 7ths with the bass) and so do not belong to the harmony: they are decorating the melodic line.

Telemann: *Gavotte en Rondeau* (1732–3)

Arne (*c*.1756)

Three parts

◆ In three-part textures it is possible to include more of the notes of the chord. Even so, notice how extra notes are added for emphasis (shown by asterisks) to the cadences in the examples below.

Exercise 79   Play through the following extracts and label the chords marked with an asterisk.

Apart from some contrapuntal forms, in which the number of voices is fixed, the texture of much music varies in the course of the composition. Classical composers, in particular, would present a succession of contrasting ideas, varying the thickness of the texture.

Exercise 80 In the opening of Mozart's Piano Sonata in B♭, K570 (below) you can see the different textures of the harmony. Play through the extract and then comment briefly on each bracketed section (a)–(f) and the musical material used. Label the chords implied or stated at the asterisks.

Mozart: Piano Sonata in B♭, K570 (1789)

PART 3

EXTENDED PROGRESSIONS

The Progression of 5ths

CHAPTER 9

So far, our consideration of chord progressions has focused on cadences, the 'punctuation marks' of music. Cadences consist essentially of two chords, most frequently V–I, the perfect cadence, and I–V, the imperfect cadence. We have seen that V may be decorated with Ic to give the common progression known as the cadential $^6_4$.

By now you will have recognized the importance of the harmonic relationship of V–I. In this progression, the root of V moves down a 5th or up a 4th to I.

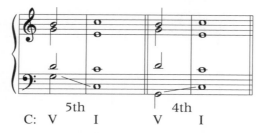

The relationship is important not just at cadences, though, but often throughout a musical phrase. We can extend the principle further, and form a progression in which the roots of all but one of the chords share the same relationship. The exception is the move from IV to vii° (F to B in C major), which features a **diminished 5th** rather than the perfect intervals between all the other root notes.

- ◆ This sequence is known as the **progression (or cycle) of 5ths**. We can see that the bass line moves in a strong sequence of rising 4ths or falling 5ths that includes all the triads in the key.
- ◆ It is a very lively and satisfying progression that appears with extraordinary diversity throughout the tonal period.

Here is a characteristic example:

Vivaldi: Concerto for Flute and Strings, *The Goldfinch*, Op. 10 No. 3 (*c*.1728)

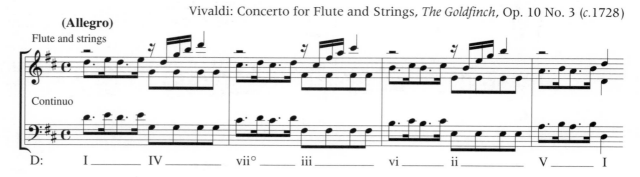

The basic progression

Major key

- ◆ In a major key the sequence of chords is as follows:

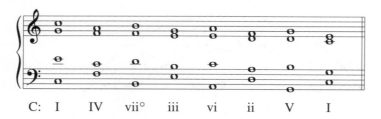

Look at the bass line to see the V–I principle at work. The sequence ends with a perfect cadence, V–I. Working backwards:

- the root of ii (D) is V of chord V (G);
- the root of vi (A) is V of chord ii (D);
- the root of iii (E) is V of chord vi (A);
- the root of vii° (B) is V of chord iii (E);
- the root of IV (F) is ♭V of chord vii° (B);
- the root of I (C) is V of chord IV (F).

Exercises   81   Complete these patterns for keyboard and label the chords. Play them through and learn the sequence from memory in as many keys as you can manage.

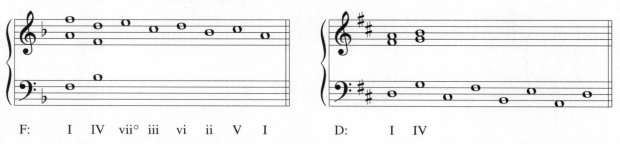

F: I   IV   vii°   iii   vi   ii   V   I   D: I   IV

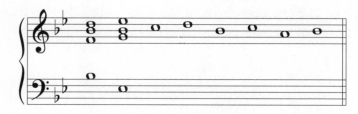

B♭:

82   Continue the following sequences, based on the progression of 5ths. Label the chords.

G:

F:

Experiment with other figurations, either writing them down or trying them out at the piano. In practice, composers would often vary the shapes in such sequences to create a more satisfying melody.

Minor key

◆ In a minor key the sequence of chords is as follows:

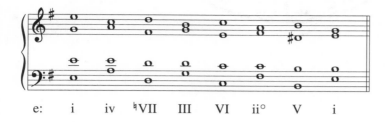

e: i   iv ♮VII III VI ii° V i

(Fast, lively)

Borée [𝄿]   Richard Jones (1732)

e: i   iv ♮VII III VI ii⁽°⁾ V i

harmonic outline

e: i   iv ♮VII III VI ii⁽°⁾ V i

Notice that:

◆ ♮VII is built on the **flattened** leading note;

◆ chords ♮VII, III, VI (and V) are major in a minor key.

Exercises

83 Complete these progressions for keyboard and label the chords. Play them through and learn the pattern from memory in as many keys as you can manage.

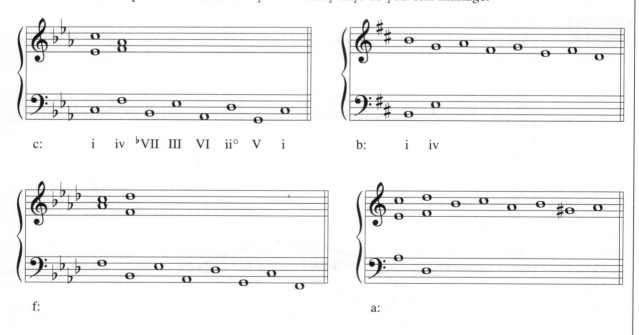

c: i iv ♭VII III VI ii° V i   b: i iv

f: a:

84   Continue these sequences based on the progression of 5ths and label the chords.

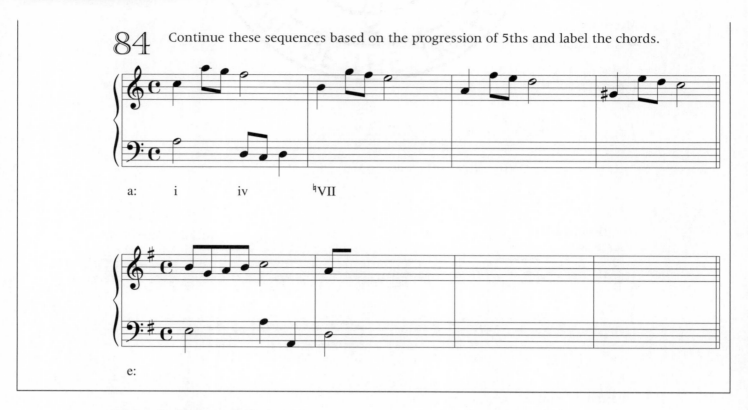

a: i   iv   ♮VII

e:

Chords in inversion

◆ Some of the chords in the progression may be in inversions.

Handel: *Sept pièces* (1733)

Chaconne

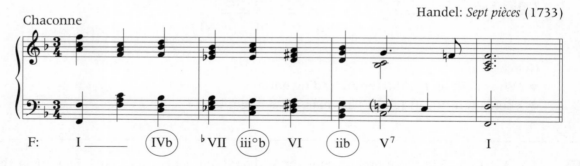

F: I _____   IVb   ♭VII   iii°b   VI   iib   V⁷   I

Exercise

85   Label the chords, some of which are in inversion, in the following extracts. Complete the bass line where necessary.

Bach: Toccata and Fugue in D minor (*c.*1708)

d: i   ib   iv   9   8

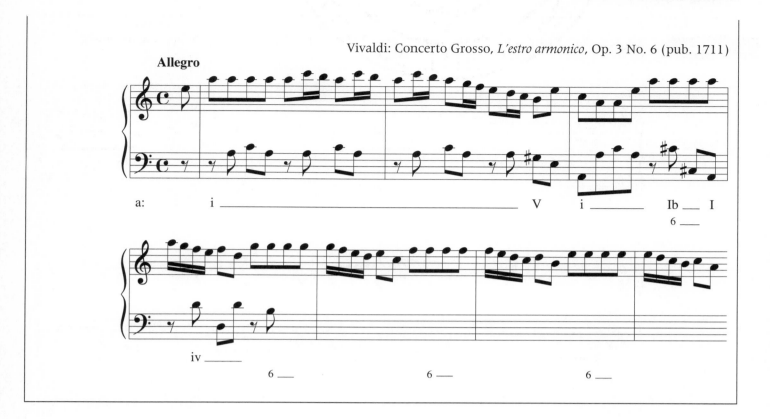

Vivaldi: Concerto Grosso, *L'estro armonico*, Op. 3 No. 6 (pub. 1711)

Approaching the cadence

The basic cadential formula of much music in the tonal period is vi–ii–V–I in a major key (VI–ii°–V–i in a minor key). As you can see, this is the last part of the progression of 5ths, and it is the commonest instance of the pattern.

Here is a characteristic example:

Clérambault: *Premier livre de pièces de clavecin* (1704)

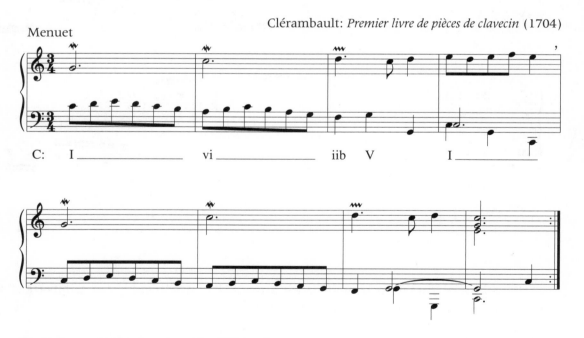

Notice here and in the examples below that:
- in the approach to V, chord ii (ii° in a minor key) is more often found in first inversion – iib;
- V is often decorated by Ic (ic), especially in the Classical period (*see* Chapter 7);
- iib may be preceded by I or Ib, rather than vi.

Exercise 86   Label the chords in the following extracts, noting the use of these approach chords.

Handel: *The Water Music* (1717)

C. P. E. Bach: *Little Notebook for Anna Magdalena Bach* (c.1722)

In the Classical period particularly, such strong, definite cadences were important since they clarified the tonal centres or keys in the sections of a piece.

Exercise 87 Label the asterisked chords in the following extracts by Beethoven and Mozart. Note how the descending bass line in the Beethoven example creates a particularly satisfying progression.

Beethoven: Piano Concerto No. 3 in C minor, Op. 37 (*c*.1800)

Mozart: Serenade in G, *Eine kleine Nachtmusik*, K525 (1787)

◆ In the nineteenth century composers continued to base their harmony on the progression of 5ths and other strong functional chord progressions. In the interest of expression, however, textures became ever more elaborate, with increasing harmonic and melodic decoration (*see* Part 5).

Chopin: Nocturne in C minor, Op. 48 No. 1 (1837)

Liszt: Piano Sonata in B minor (1852–3)

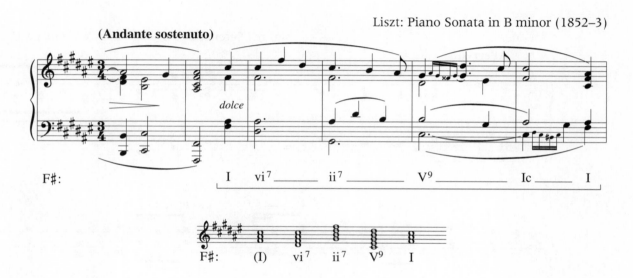

◆ The sound of this cadential sequence based on the progression of 5ths should now be familiar to you. The following exercise will help you develop your harmonic skill and part-writing.

Exercise   **88**   Complete these cadence phrases from various carols for SATB. Check for consecutives as you go.

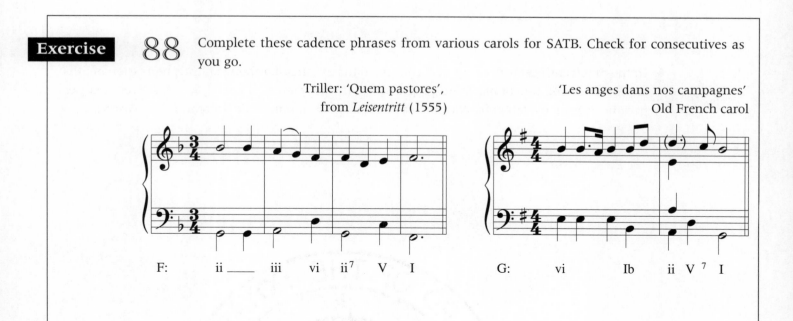

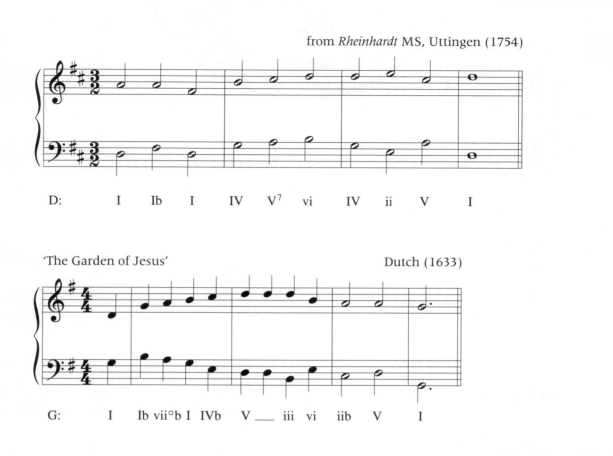

from *Rheinhardt* MS, Uttingen (1754)

D: I   Ib   I   IV   V⁷   vi   IV   ii   V   I

'The Garden of Jesus'   Dutch (1633)

G: I   Ib vii°b I IVb   V ___ iii   vi   iib   V   I

The addition of 7ths

We saw in Chapter 6 that 7ths can be added to any triad. In the case of the dominant triad, V, the result is a chord that tends strongly to resolve to the tonic chord. When a 7th is added to other triads, even minor and diminished ones, a similar tendency will exist to resolve to a chord whose root is a 5th away. This need for individual notes to resolve in certain directions propels the music forward.

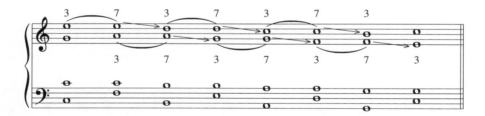

Notice that:
- each 7th is **prepared**, that is, it occurs as a consonance in the previous chord;
- each 7th falls by step in the same part.

Remember that:
- consonant intervals include all major and minor 3rds and 6ths and perfect octaves and 5ths;
- dissonant intervals include all 2nds, 9ths, 4ths and 7ths.

The principle of preparing dissonances to sound on strong beats has existed since the Renaissance period (*c.*1400–1580) and is by now a 'fact of history'. Bach and Handel certainly maintained the principle, as did later composers to a lesser extent (we will deal with this further in Chapter 14).

Exercises

89 Complete these chains of 7ths in the progression of 5ths.

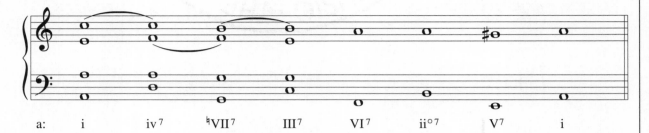

a: i   iv⁷   ♮VII⁷   III⁷   VI⁷   ii°⁷   V⁷   i

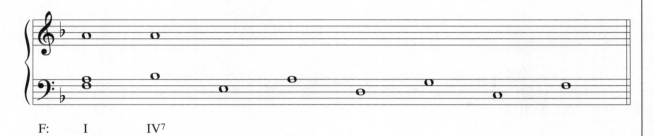

F: I   IV⁷

90 Work out some sequential patterns to decorate the following basic progression. The start of one is given for you. On the keyboard, try out this and other patterns in different keys.

a:

91 Label the chords in the following extracts.

Vivaldi: Concerto Grosso, *L'estro armonico*, Op. 3 No. 8 (pub. 1711)

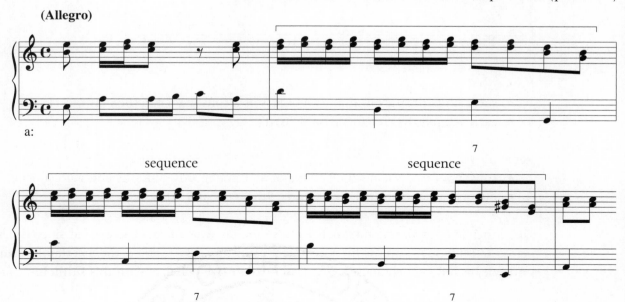

- Composers often added 7ths only to alternate chords in a progression of 5ths, as in the Vivaldi extract.
- You will notice that the recurring bass pattern in the progression of 5ths is usually matched by sequential patterns in the upper parts. Much Baroque music features such sequences, often very elaborately. Vivaldi especially delighted in using them.

Chord ii⁷(b)

If a 7th is added to chord ii, the cadential progression we have discussed above (ii–V–I) becomes stronger still. As with the triad on ii, ii⁷ is usually heard in first inversion, as ii⁷b.

- Remember that the 7th should normally be prepared and resolved downwards in the same part.
- As with the triad on ii, ii⁷b may be preceded by I or Ib (*b*), rather than vi (*a*).

Play these progressions and examples:

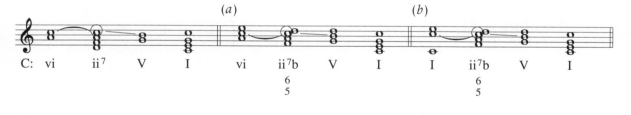

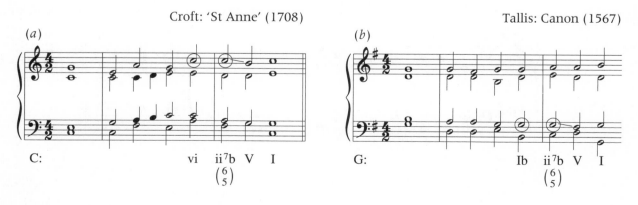

Exercises 92   Here is an elaboration of the same progression from Mozart's Piano Sonata in A minor, K310. Continue the labelling.

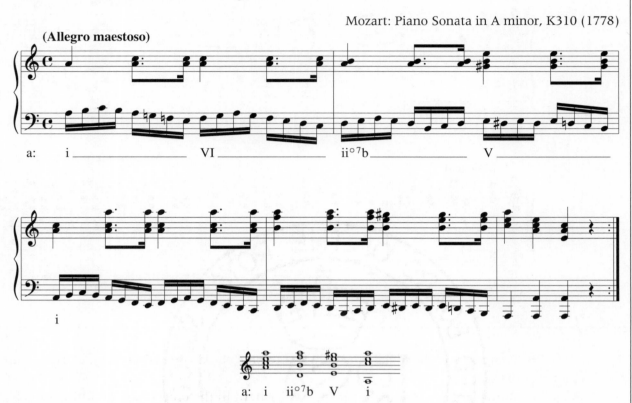

Mozart: Piano Sonata in A minor, K310 (1778)

93   Complete the harmony of these cadential phrases from various psalters for SATB.

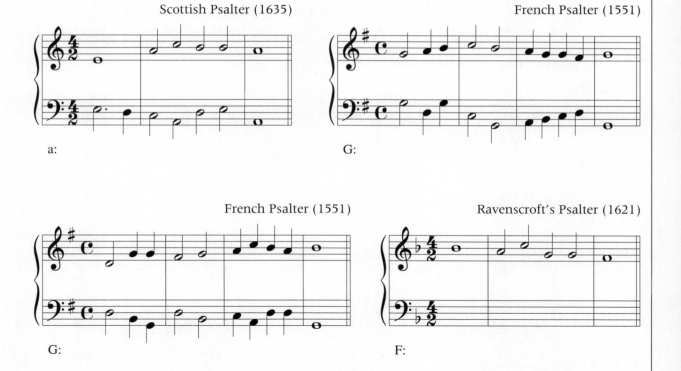

Scottish Psalter (1635)

French Psalter (1551)

French Psalter (1551)

Ravenscroft's Psalter (1621)

94   Complete these chorale phrases for SATB using the chords indicated. Check for consecutives and add the figuring.

The complete progression – the sequence

◆ The complete progression of 5ths is not as common as the cadential formula vi–ii–V–I (VI–ii°–V–i), but it is found in a great deal of Baroque music, especially in a sequence.

◆ It is useful to memorize the order of the progression:
   Major key: I–IV–vii°–iii–vi–ii–V–I
   Minor key: i–iv–♭VII–III–VI–ii°–V–i

By now, you should be able to recognize the characteristic sound of the progression, especially following the bass line with the ear and the eye.

◆ Leaps in the bass line and repeated or sequential patterns in the upper parts should alert you to the progression.

◆ When you hear chord I move to IV (i–iv), especially in a Baroque piece, it probably indicates the beginning of the full progression.

Exercise 95 Play through the following extracts and label the progression of 5ths in each. In the Bach Chaconne the progression appears three times, as shown.

Bach: Concerto, from Cantata 142 *Uns ist ein Kind geboren* (1712)

Weiss: *Sonata per il Liuto*, No. 7 (*c*.1740)

Menuet I

Bach: French Suite No. 3 in B minor (1722–5)

b:

Chaconne

Bach: Partita No. 2 in D minor for Unaccompanied Violin (1720)

d:

In the extract from Bach's French Suite in B minor, notice that the progression of 5ths continues, although the melodic sequence does not. The melodic line often changes at the approach to a cadence.

Exercise $\quad$ 96 $\quad$ Continue these sequences in the progression of 5ths. Label the chords. Notice that some chords may appear in inversion and contain 7ths. When you have finished, play through the extracts.

Corelli: Trio Sonata, Op. 1 No. 4 (1683)

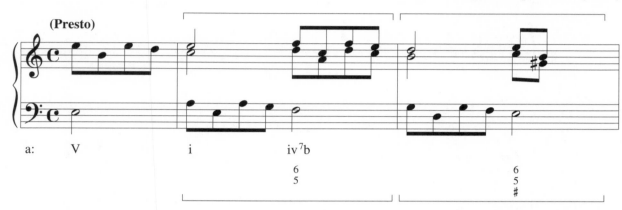

Corelli: Trio Sonata, Op. 1 No. 4 (1683)

Corelli: Trio Sonata, Op. 1 No. 6 (1683)

Corelli: Trio Sonata, Op. 1 No. 5 (1683)

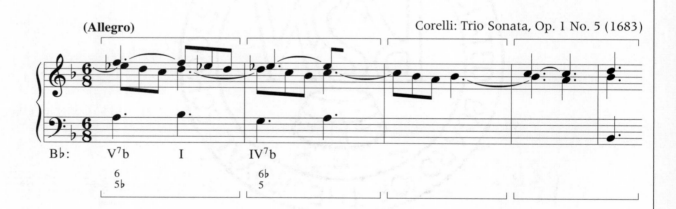

† Note the hemiola.

Bach: Partita No. 3 in A minor for keyboard (1731)

Fantasia

Bach: French Suite No. 2 in C minor (1722–5)

Menuet I

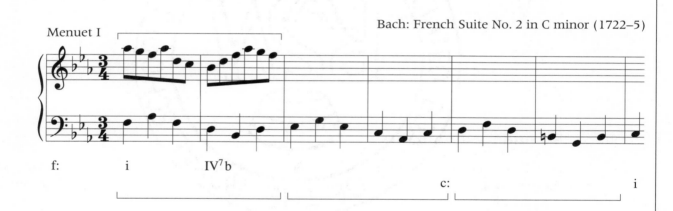

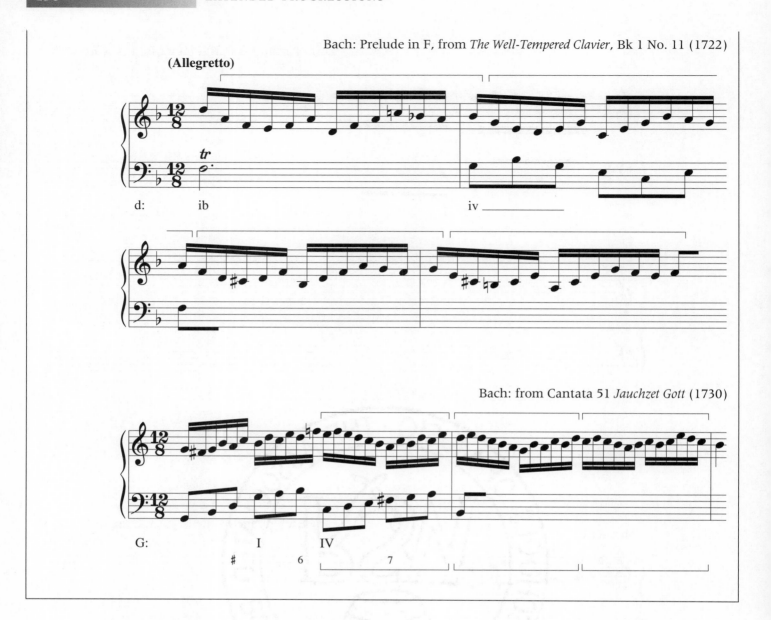

Bach: Prelude in F, from *The Well-Tempered Clavier*, Bk 1 No. 11 (1722)

Bach: from Cantata 51 *Jauchzet Gott* (1730)

Secondary dominants

One final modification of the progression needs to be mentioned because it is an aspect of the progression of 5ths. However, students may prefer to cover this section after 'Modulation' in Chapter 12.

◆ Minor and diminished chords in a progression are sometimes altered to major so that they become **real** dominant 7ths of the next chord, and the sharpened 3rd becomes a kind of leading note. Such an altered chord is called a **secondary dominant**.

Here is the progression in C major, chromatically altered in this way:

C: I   I^{b7} IV^{b7} VII^7 III^7 VI^7 II^7 V^7 I

◆ In practice, composers will usually alter only a few chords. Here are two examples from the keyboard works of Bach, in which the chromatically altered chords in a modulating sequence have been asterisked.

Bach: Partita No. 5 in G (1731)

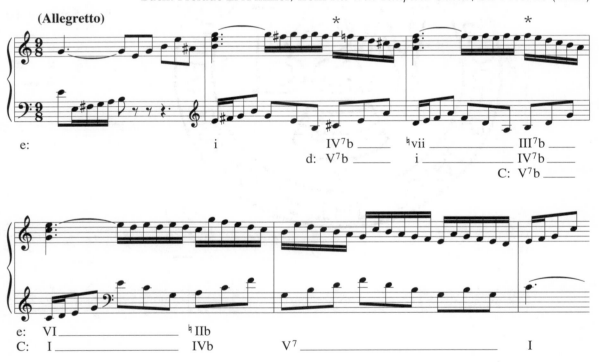

Bach: Prelude in A minor, from *The Well-Tempered Clavier*, Bk 1 No. 20 (1722)

The progression of 5ths, then, is an extremely important chord pattern in tonal music. The formula of the progression is often reflected in the sequential nature of the music built upon it. Each period in musical history has created characteristic sequence shapes, and you will find many examples in the pieces you are learning to play. The exercise below shows examples of the progression ranging from the Baroque era to the twentieth century.

Jazz performers will realize that the ii–V–I progression is a basic feature of the music they play.

Exercise $\mathcal{97}$ Play through the following extracts and note the various examples of the progression of 5ths. Label the progression and bracket any sequences.

Bach: French Suite No. 1 in D minor (1722–5)

Menuet II

d:

d:

Mozart: Piano Sonata in B♭, K333 (1778)

(Allegretto grazioso)

c: V⁷b _____   i _____ (7)   IV⁷b

c:

Schubert: 'Wanderer' Fantasy, Op. 15 (1822)

Brahms: Intermezzo, Op. 117 No. 2 (1892)

Andante non troppo e con molto espressione

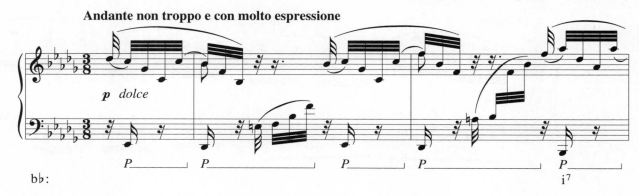

Tchaikovsky: *Romeo and Juliet* (1880)

Ravel: *Pavane pour une infante défunte* (1899–1905)

Although the later examples elaborate the sequence melodically and harmonically, you will find that the underlying chord sequence remains clear.

Chord Groups –
the Subdominant Family

CHAPTER 10

Some revision and some new ideas

We have already identified the tonic (I) and dominant (V) as the most important chords in the key, and we have seen how the others form the **progression of 5ths**. Chords in tonal music turn out to have a clear hierarchy. Each has its specific function in the key and can behave accordingly. A piece will characteristically open by establishing the tonic key with chord I. Then the music will generally move to one of the group of chords associated with the **subdominant**: ii, IV and vi. The next move will be to a chord in the dominant group (*see* Chapter 6) – V, vii, (iii) – which leads back to the tonic, I.

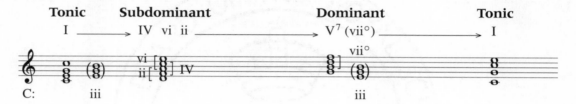

We have seen this principle at work in the approach to the cadence (Chapter 9, p. 121):

| iii | vi | ii | V | I |
| I | vi | ii | V | I |

and in the complete progression of 5ths (Chapter 9, p. 130):

| I | IV | vii° | iii | vi | ii | V | I |

Here is the opening of a keyboard prelude in C, attributed to Bach, which shows this fundamental progression of tonic–subdominant–dominant–tonic over a pedal note:

Bach: Prelude in C, BWV 939 (*c*.1720)

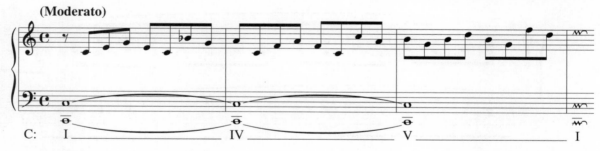

There will of course always be exceptions to this formula, but it holds good for a significant amount of tonal music. One exception regularly encountered is where chords succeed each other in first inversion in a rising or falling scale pattern. In that case, they can appear in any order:

Mozart: 'The March of the Priests', from *The Magic Flute* (1791)

F: Ib   iib iiib IVb vib   Vb V⁷   I

Chord IV

◆ Chord IV is the third primary triad in the key, with I and V, but it has none of the musical 'thrust' of the dominant chord.

◆ It is found in the plagal cadence (IV–I) where it confirms the tonic key, creating a sense of repose or a 'winding down' in the musical action (*see* Chapter 5). It often appears over a tonic pedal, as in this example, forming a second inversion:

Bach: Prelude in A, from *The Well-Tempered Clavier*, Bk 2 No. 19 (1744)

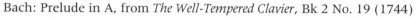

A:

IVc _____ I

◆ It can precede chord V in an imperfect cadence, though I or ii(b) are more usual.

Rouget de Lisle: *La Marseillaise* (1792)

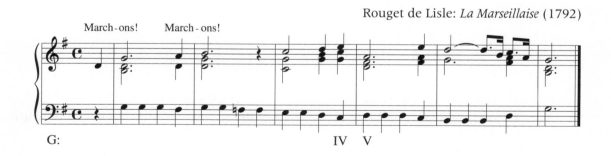

March-ons!   March-ons!

G: IV   V

◆ In second inversion it can act as an auxiliary chord to chord I, when it moves by step away from and back to the original chord in the progression I–IVc–I (*see* Chapter 7, p. 100, where some examples are given). Chord IV also appears with chord I in the passing $^6_4$ progression (*see* p. 98).

Chord IV can sometimes appear chromatically altered to give a different 'colouring':

1   As a minor chord in a major key, i.e. chord iv.

Exercise 98   Identify chord iv in the following extracts.

2   As a diminished 7th of the dominant, $^\sharp$iv^{d7} (*see* Chapter 6, p. 84).

3   As the 'Italian' and 'German' versions of the augmented 6th chord, both of which derive from chord IV.

($^\sharp$iv^{d7} and augmented 6th chords are discussed in Chapter 15.)

Chord ii

◆ The bass note of chord ii (II) is the dominant of the dominant, hence its importance in the progression of 5ths (*see* Chapter 9).

◆ The addition of a 7th creates a stronger effect.

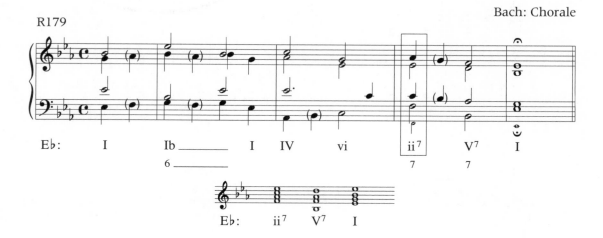

◆ In a minor key, ii° is normally heard as a diminished triad. Like chord vii°, therefore, it will normally appear in first inversion with either the bass note, the 3rd, doubled (*a*), or with an added 7th (*b*):

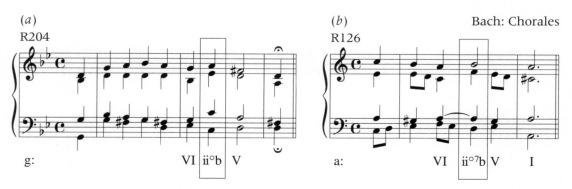

◆ As we have seen with chord IV, chord ii may be chromatically altered. A characteristic modification is to sharpen the 3rd, making the chord major instead of minor, and sometimes to add a 7th. This makes the chord sound like a genuine dominant or dominant 7th of the dominant, V. This so-called secondary dominant strengthens the cadential progression (*see* Chapter 9, p. 136).

Exercise 99 Complete chord II⁷b in the following extracts.

Bach: Chorales

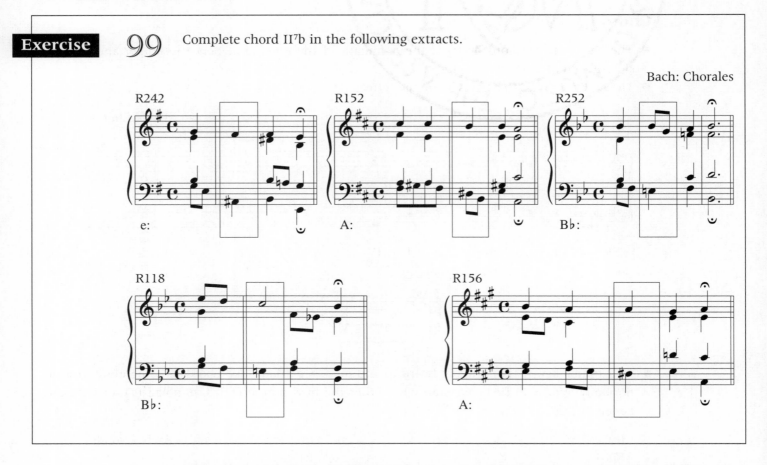

- Other altered versions of ii include the 'Neapolitan 6th' (♭IIb) and the version of the augmented 6th chord known as the 'French 6th'. These are discussed in Chapter 15.

Chord vi

- Chord vi often follows chord V to form an interrupted cadence (*see* Chapter 5). Though such a cadence is usually a musical surprise, even a dramatic gesture, it does not normally stop the flow.

- Like chords IV and ii, chord vi is sometimes chromatically altered. In a major key, the interrupted cadence may end with a major chord built on the **flattened** sixth degree of the scale, ♭VI, sometimes with an added 7th. In a minor key, the triad built on the flattened sixth degree is a major chord anyway, and so needs no alteration.

Schubert: Symphony No. 5 in B♭ (1816)

- Chord vi characteristically comes between iii and ii in the progression of 5ths. In the shortened cadential form of the progression it can appear as one of the approach chords (*see* Chapter 9).

- The first inversion is used very rarely and should normally be avoided. Mozart created a rather special interrupted cadence with this chord at the end of the 'Rex tremendae' from his *Requiem*.

Mozart: 'Rex tremendae', from *Requiem* (1791)

(For other altered versions of chord vi, *see* Chapter 15.)

Summary

So, we have seen that music commonly moves **away** from chord I to the subdominant family of chords, sometimes via chord iii. It then moves towards the dominant group, which may be decorated in various ways, and from here the music returns to I.

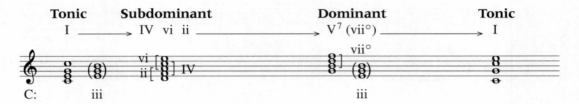

This is a very common sequence of moves. However, note that:

- *some of the strongest and most satisfying passages in tonal music involve tonic (I) and dominant (V) chords **only**, the final chords of the progression of 5ths;*

- IV may move **back** to I in a plagal cadence;

- I may move to V in an imperfect cadence;

- although iii is often found between I and IV, and between vii° and vi in the progression of 5ths, it can also be a substitute for the dominant, as iiib, resolving to I (*see* Chapter 6, p. 86);

- chords can break the mould in a pattern of first inversion chords, which are free to move up and down the scale in any order.

◆ Therefore progressions such as the following are not common **in the tonal period** and should be used with care:

ii–I;   VI–I;   V–IV;   V–ii

You will find it a great help in your harmonization and analysis work if you bear in mind this hierarchy and the groupings that we have looked at. Handling chord progressions becomes much simpler if the music is seen to move according to clearly defined principles.

Scale Movement

CHAPTER 11

Many tonal melodies move by step or contain passages of scale movement. We will therefore look in this chapter at how to harmonize scale passages, and we will also consider the way composers have harmonized scale movement when it appears in the bass line.

With scale movement, a composer has the choice of (*a*) harmonizing each note of the scale (normally the case in hymns and chorales), or (*b*) reducing the number of chords and treating some notes in the scale as passing and auxiliary notes (the notes ringed below):

Piae Cantiones (1582)

Scale movement in a major key

◆ In an ascending scale chords often alternate between I and V or I and IV.
◆ A descending scale will sometimes take iii and vi.
◆ The cadences follow established patterns, such as I(b) or VI, followed by iib–Ic–V–I (descending) or IV–V–I (ascending).

Exercises

100   Harmonize this scale using the chords suggested.

D: I   V   I   IVb   Ib   IV   V   I

D: I   iii   IV   I   iib   Ic   V   I
           or V   vi   Ib
     or vi   III   IV   I

101   Experiment at the keyboard to find alternative harmonizations and write them down.

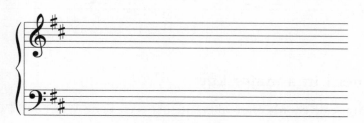

D:

D:

102 Harmonize these phrases in scale movement. Use the harmonies already suggested, or
     work out your own.

F: V   G: D: I

Bb: Ib   A: V   a: I
                              6   6

103   Label the chords in these extracts, and note the harmonies that Bach, Handel and Beethoven use.

R20   Bach: Chorale

Handel: 'Hallelujah Chorus', from *Messiah* (1742)

Beethoven: Piano Sonata in C, Op. 53 'Waldstein' (1803–4)

Tranquillo

Scale movement in a minor key

◆ Melodies usually use the melodic minor scale, because the harmonic minor contains the awkward interval of an augmented 2nd between the sixth and seventh degrees. The ascending and descending forms of the melodic minor scale are different, though, so they require different harmonies.

◆ The sixth and seventh degrees of the ascending melodic minor scale are sharpened, forming a major 6th and major 7th with the tonic. The sixth degree is often harmonized by chord iv with its 3rd altered to the major form, i.e. IV. For example:

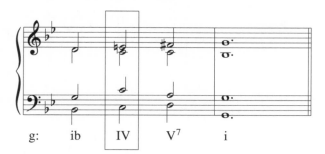

g: ib   IV   V⁷   i

◆ Where the raised sixth and seventh degrees appear in the bass, chord IV⁷b is sometimes used (marked * in *Exercise 104* below).

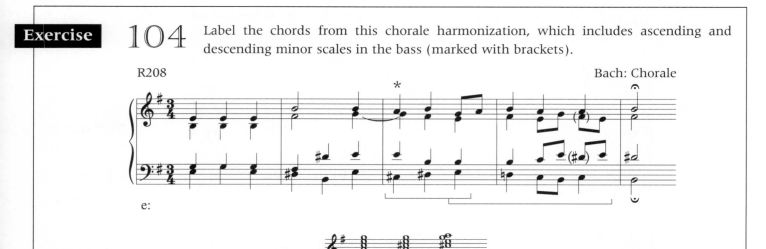

Exercise 104   Label the chords from this chorale harmonization, which includes ascending and descending minor scales in the bass (marked with brackets).

R208   Bach: Chorale

e:

e: iv⁷   IV⁷   IV⁷b

◆ Chord IV⁷d is also found:

R228   Bach: Chorale

a: V   ib   IV⁷d   vii°b   i   V

◆ The sixth and seventh degrees of the descending melodic minor scale form a minor 7th and minor 6th with the tonic. It is often desirable to introduce the sharpened leading note as soon as possible after the minor seventh degree, in order to reinforce the sense of key:

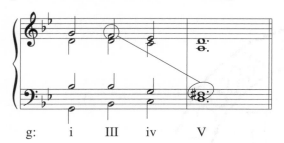

g: i   III   iv   V

Exercises

105   Harmonize this scale using the chords suggested.

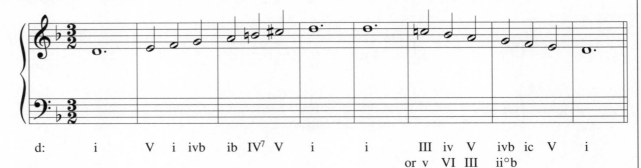

d: i   V   i   ivb   ib IV⁷ V   i   i   III   iv   V   ivb ic V   i
                                                                          or v   VI   III   ii°b

106   Experiment at the keyboard to find alternative harmonizations and write them down.

107   Complete in four parts the various scale passages below and add figuring.

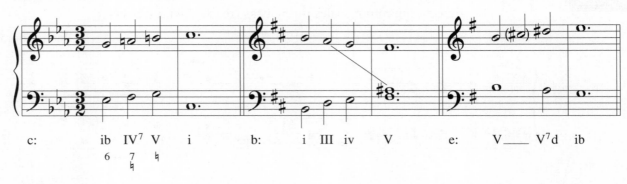

c: ib IV⁷ V   i   b: i III iv   V   e: V___ V⁷d ib
            6   7   ♮
                 ♮

d: i   vb   ivb   V   V ___ V⁷b   i   III⁺b IV⁷b V⁷b   i

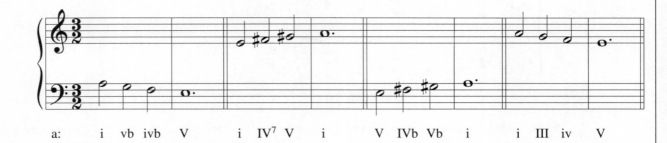

a: i   vb   ivb   V   i IV⁷ V   i   V IVb Vb   i   i III iv   V

e: i IV⁷ V   i   V V⁷d ib vii°b i   vb   ivb   V   i III iv   V

108 Consider the examples below and label the chords in the bracketed sections.

R213

Bach: Chorale

d:

Sweelinck: Variations on *Mein junges Leben hat ein End* (?c.1610)

d:

Purcell: 'With drooping wings ye Cupids come', from *Dido and Aeneas* (1689)

g:

The passing $\frac{6}{4}$

We saw in Chapter 7 (page 98) how in this progression the second inversion chord occurs on a weak beat, 'sandwiched' between two other chords:

I–V$^{(7)}$c–Ib or Ib–V$^{(7)}$c–I

IV–Ic–IVb or IVb–Ic–IV

Exercise 109   Identify the chords in the bracketed phrases below. The scale movement may sometimes occur in the bass, and the $\frac{6}{4}$ chord may appear on a strong beat:

Beethoven: Symphony No. 2 in D (1801–2)

D:

Beethoven: Symphony No. 3 in E♭, 'Eroica' (1803)

f:

Tchaikovsky: 'The Sick Doll', from *Album for the Young*, Op. 39 No. 7 (1878)

g:

◆ The passing $\frac{6}{4}$ **can** also be found, though less commonly, between two **different** chords. A line that contains consecutively the fourth, third and second degrees of the scale may be harmonized by IVb–Ic–ii⁷b. Here is a characteristic example from one of Bach's chorales in the minor key:

R263   Bach: Chorale

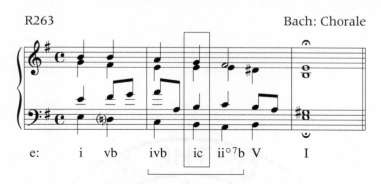

e: i   vb   ivb   ic   ii°⁷b   V   I

Exercises 110   Label and figure the bracketed chords in these extracts.

Bach: Chorales

111   Complete these passing $^6_4$ progressions using the chords indicated. Add the figuring and play them through.

     Remember to:

- double the **bass** note of the $^6_4$;
- prepare the 7th of chord ii⁷b (*see* Chapter 9, p. 127).

Bach: Chorales

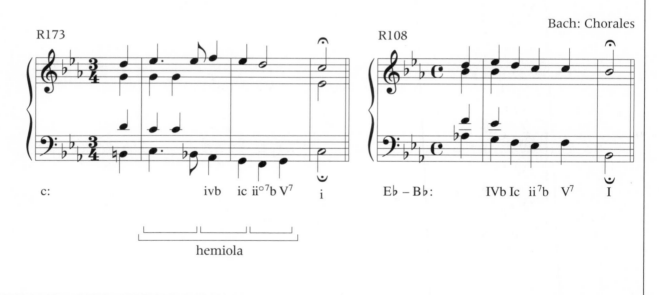

So, the passing $^6_4$ in its various forms can be used to harmonize stepwise movement. Remember that the passing $^6_3$ can also be used.

Movement in $\frac{6}{3}$ chords

We saw in Chapter 3, page 27 that strings of $\frac{6}{3}$ chords were common in the tonal era, especially in Baroque music.

Exercise 112   Complete the harmony in the following extracts and label and figure the chords. Play through the completed passages to familiarize yourself with the sound of the progression. Add a second violin part only to the two Corelli extracts.

Bach: Chorales

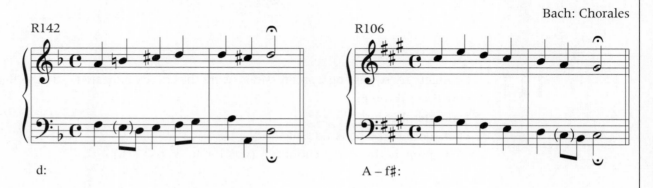

Corelli: Trio Sonata, Op. 1 No. 7 (1683)

Corelli: Trio Sonata, Op. 2 No. 8 (1685)

Scale movement in the bass

We have looked at examples in which the bass line shadows stepwise movement in the top part. However, composers throughout the tonal period used scale passages in the bass part alone, and it makes for particularly satisfying progressions.

Exercises 113 Play through the following extracts, noting the effect of the ascending and descending bass lines. Label the chords used.

Bach: 'Sanctus', from Mass in B minor (1747–9)

D:

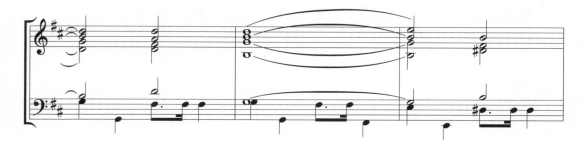

Elgar: Theme from *Variations on an Original Theme (Enigma)*, Op. 36 (1899)

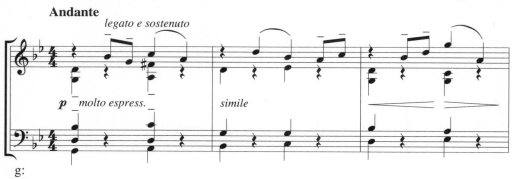

g:

114

Review the work you have done in this chapter by realizing for SATB the following figured bass passages which contain scale movement.

The notes that are not part of the harmony are in brackets.

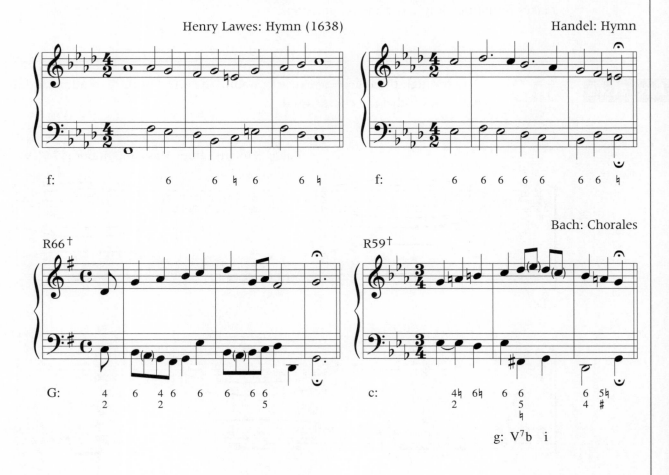

† From '69 Chorale Melodies with Figured Bass' from G. C. Schemelli's *Gesangbuch* (published 1736).

PART 4

MODULATION

Modulation – its Purpose and Practice

CHAPTER 12

Establishing the tonic key

A piece of music that remained in the same key throughout would soon lose interest. Almost all pieces composed in the tonal period, even short ones, change key, or **modulate**, at some point. Modulation is in fact one of the most important 'incidents' in tonal music, providing contrast, variety, colour and drama in the music.

In this chapter and the next we will examine the process of modulation and how composers have used it. But before that, we will look briefly at how a key is established in the first place.

As the name suggests, the basis of tonal music is the key or tonal centre, and asserting that centre is of great importance.

The strongest progressions that we have looked at so far, such as the V⁷–I cadence or the progression of 5ths, move towards a tonic chord. Although a passage in tonal music may be temporarily ambiguous, so that one is briefly not sure **which** key the music is in, it never completely loses a sense of key. The home key of a piece is the base from which it starts and to which it usually returns. The important musical structures of the tonal period, such as ritornello or sonata forms, express this overall attachment to a key centre. In the **smaller** units of the musical phrase, strong progressions may confirm the home key or **modulate** to new tonal centres.

◆ The tonic key may be asserted simply by reiterating chord I which, as we know, is built on the key note. Here are the last bars of Beethoven's Symphony No. 3, 'Eroica':

Beethoven: Symphony No. 3 in E♭, 'Eroica' (1803)

◆ There is often a tonic pedal note in the opening and closing bars of movements, instilling in the listener's mind the sensation of the tonic or 'home' key. Here are the opening and closing bars of the first movement of Beethoven's Piano Sonata in E♭, Op. 7:

Beethoven: Piano Sonata in E♭, Op. 7 (1796–7)

opening bars

closing bars

◆ The dominant chord is also very important in establishing the home key. The dominant chord leads strongly to the tonic, as we have seen, and the V⁷–I perfect cadence is one of the most important progressions in the whole of tonal music.

◆ The dominant chord may alternate with chord I, the repeated perfect cadence, serving to strengthen the tonal centre.

Exercise 115   In the following extract identify the chords marked with an asterisk as I (i) or V^(7), and note the different ways in which these chords may be expressed.

Beethoven: Piano Sonata in F minor, Op. 2 No. 1 (1795)

f: i   V⁷

◆ In the exercise above, notice the acceleration of the harmonic rhythm at the approach to the cadence.

◆ The alternation of chords I and V is frequently used repeatedly at the end of a piece to bring the music to a firm conclusion in the home key.

Exercise **116** Label the chords marked with an asterisk in the following extract.

Beethoven: Symphony No. 5 in C minor, Op. 67 (1808)

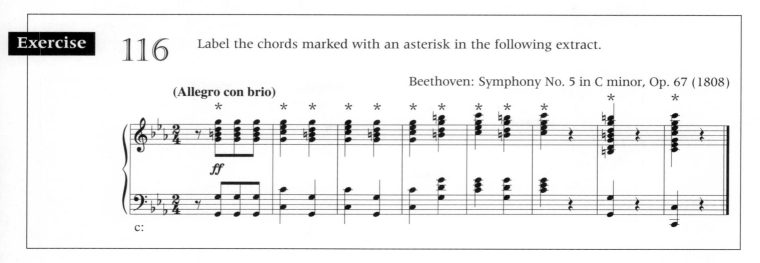

◆ It is common to begin with an upbeat, or **anacrusis**, usually of chord V, which leads to chord I on the downbeat.

Exercise **117** Label the alternating tonic and dominant chords in this extract.

Beethoven: Piano Sonata in A♭, Op. 26 (1800–01)

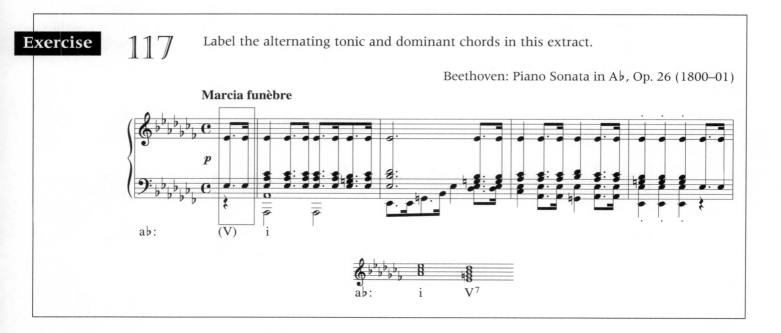

◆ A pedal note on the dominant leads us to expect the tonic. Notice how firmly the following prelude ends with a V⁷–I cadence in the tonic **major**, even after the rich minor harmonies over a dominant pedal. The practice of ending a piece in the minor key with a strong tonic **major** chord, the so-called *tierce de Picardie*, had become an established convention by Bach's day.

Bach: Prelude in F minor, from *The Well-Tempered Clavier*, Bk 1 No. 12 (1722)

◆ Lastly, it should be noted that the first chord in a piece was not always chord I. Beethoven and other nineteenth-century composers sometimes made the listener wait for confirmation of the home key. The following extract starts expectantly with chord ii⁷b, then moves up by semitones through a mysterious diminished 7th chord (♯iv^d7) to arrive at the home chord of Ic and the cadence V–I.

Beethoven: Piano Sonata in E♭, Op. 31 No. 3 (1802)

The purpose of modulation

In tonal music modulation serves two functions:

- **to give interest by providing contrast** with the tonic or home key, either briefly, in a phrase or section, or across a whole piece. The significance of the modulation can vary, depending on where it occurs, the speed of the music, and what prominence it is given.
- **to give structure to a composition**. The musical forms that evolved in the tonal period, especially Classical sonata form, are largely based on the principle of contrasting keys – modulation **away from** and **back to** the home key. The return of the tonic key is often the most significant moment in a whole movement, and in sonata form comes at the recapitulation.

Some points about modulation

◆ A modulation may establish the new key smoothly, the move hardly noticeable (marked * in the following example):

Beethoven: Piano Sonata in C♯ minor, Op. 27 No. 1, 'Moonlight' (1801)

◆ There may be a definite point of 'arrival', confirmed by a **cadence** in the new key:

Verdi: 'Lacrymosa', from *Requiem* (1874)

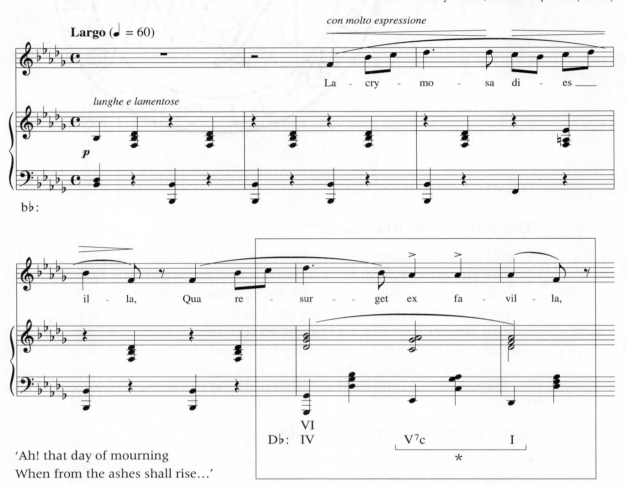

'Ah! that day of mourning
When from the ashes shall rise…'

◆ A rising or falling **sequence** may feature a modulation. However, the brief excursion in the
following extract could equally be heard as chord colouring within the tonic key. The chromatic
movement may in fact strengthen the progression.

Bach: *Little Notebook for Anna Magdalena Bach* (1722–5)

◆ An unexpected modulation may mark a **dramatic** shift:

Haydn: Piano Sonata in B♭, Hob XVI/41 (*c*.1782–4)

◆ The double bar line indicates the end of the exposition in the dominant key of F. The beginning of the development is marked by the unexpected key of D♭!

◆ Modulation may be a **means of expression**:

Schubert: 'Du bist die Ruh', Op. 59 No. 3 (1823)

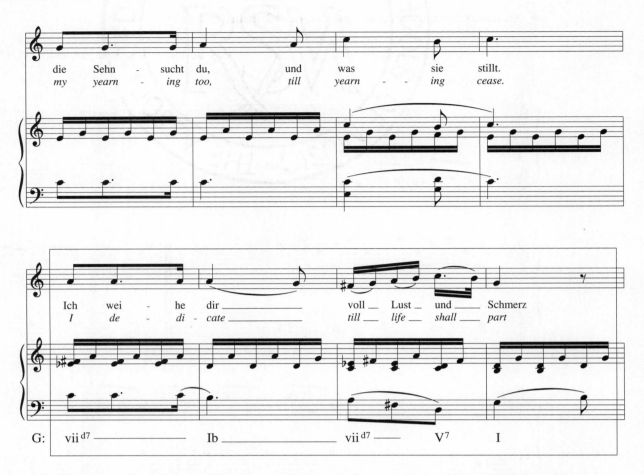

G: vii^{d7} ———————   Ib ——————   vii^{d7} ——   V⁷   I

◆ The diminished 7th, a coloured chord, creates an unexpected, poignant moment. The vii^{d7}, with its E♭, would normally lead one to expect G minor, but here it resolves to G **major**, the related (dominant) key.

Key relationships in modulation

Until about 1800 modulation was normally to the closely related keys. They are:

- keys one degree either sharp or flat of the tonic, that is, the dominant or subdominant keys and their relative minor or major keys;
- the relative major or minor of the tonic key. Minor keys move rather more frequently to the relative major than to the dominant minor.

Other keys are considered 'remote' or 'distant', and modulation to them is consequently less common.

From a major key

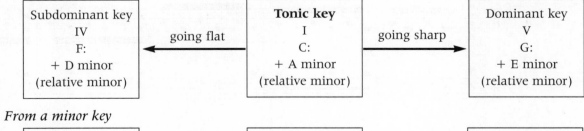

From a minor key

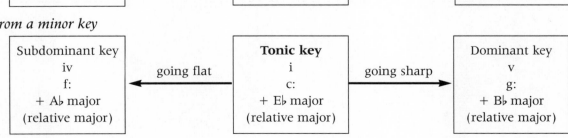

◆ 'Going sharp' means modulating to a key a 5th higher (to the dominant), that is, with one sharp more or one flat fewer in its key signature. For example, D (two sharps) to A (three sharps), or E♭ (three flats) to B♭ (two flats).

◆ 'Going flat' means modulating to a key a 5th lower or a 4th higher (to the subdominant), that is, with one flat more or one sharp fewer in its key signature. For example, E♭ (three flats) to A♭ (four flats), or D (two sharps) to G (one sharp).

When you harmonize or analyse a piece, make a note of the related keys. This will alert you to possible modulations.

Exercise 118   For practice, work out and complete the related keys for the following:

I (i)	G : e	B♭ :	E :	E♭ :	A :	b :	f :	e :	c :	d :
V (v)	D : b									
IV (iv)	C : a									

When labelling modulations:
1. indicate the initial key at the beginning of the extract, using the standard upper- or lower-case letter;
2. at the modulation, indicate the new key and its chords beneath the original key. That will enable you to show that chords represent different functions in the two keys. For example, the dominant chord (V) of the initial key may also be the tonic (I) of the new key.

Look at the examples in this chapter to familiarize yourself with this practice.

Recognizing modulation

◆ The most important clue to a modulation is the introduction of new accidentals.

◆ A new sharp (in a 'sharp' key) or a new natural (in a 'flat' key) is very likely to be a new leading note. This leading note is vital in establishing the new key. If the new key is minor the sharpened 6th from the melodic minor scale may appear as well.

◆ There may well be a cadence to confirm the new key; look at the bass line.

Consider the following example:

Este's Psalter (1592)

- ◆ At (*a*) there is a perfect cadence in the dominant key of C, indicated by the new leading note, B♮, and the V–I bass line.

- ◆ At (*b*) there is an imperfect cadence in the relative minor (D minor), indicated by the new leading note, C♯.

The new leading note will be part of one of the following:
- the dominant or dominant 7th chord in the new key;
- vii°b in the new key;
- vii^{d7} in the new key;

or occasionally,
- iiib or III⁺b in the new key.

Of these the dominant 7th is the strongest.

- ◆ A new natural (in a 'sharp' key) or a new flat (in a 'flat' key) is most likely to be the dominant 7th **note** of the new key.

Occasionally, such accidentals in tonal music are misleading. The composer may be using techniques from older music, with modal rather than tonal harmony. For example, in the chorale-like theme of the finale of Brahms's First Symphony the leading note is at first flattened, a characteristic of some modal scales. In this case the E♭ is then changed into a normal leading note, E♮.

Brahms: Symphony No. 1 in C minor (1876)

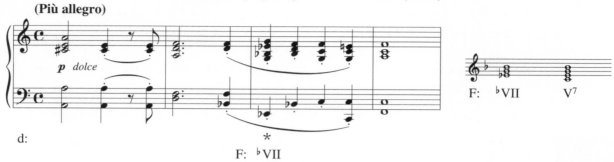

◆ New accidentals **may** simply add colour to the harmony and not change the tonal centre: see *
in the song below (*see* 'altered chords', Chapter 15).

Exercise 119 Identify the modulation in the following song. Label all the chords and circle the new
leading note and dominant 7th.

Schubert: 'Des Müllers Blumen', from *Die schöne Müllerin* (1823)

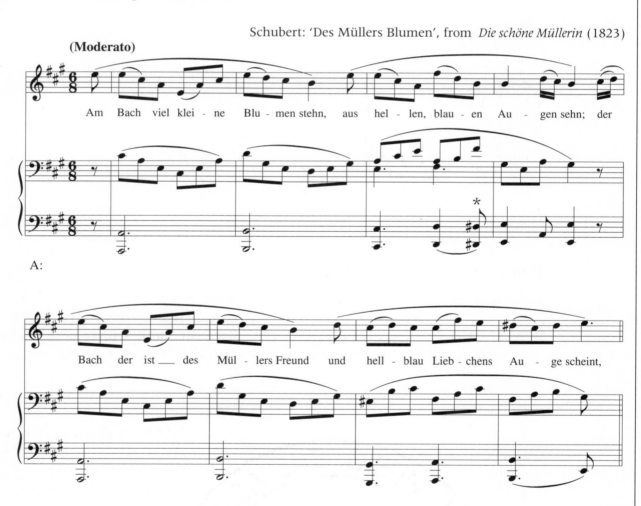

'By the brook many little flowers grow,
gazing with clear blue eyes;
The brook is the miller's friend
and my darling's eyes are bright blue,...'

◆ Note that the D♯ in bar 3 is a chromatic passing note, simply adding colour or a little 'lift' to the imperfect cadence. In the last bar it is clearly the leading note of the new key, the dominant, E. The E♯ in bar 7 is a major version of chord vi (an altered chord).

◆ As well as the dominant 7th, the **diminished 7th** chord, of the same V family, will often effect a modulation.

Exercise 120   In the following extracts the diminished 7th chord is crucial in the change of key. Complete the chord in the three examples.

Bach: Chorales

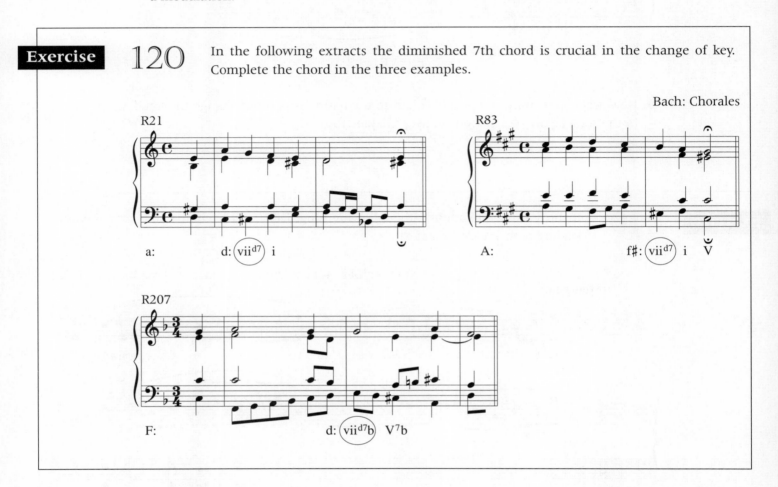

Pivot and 'abrupt' modulations

As we have noted, changes of key can be smooth or abrupt.

◆ A smooth change of key is made with the use of a **pivot chord** or **pivot note**, one that belongs to both keys. The pivot is normally followed immediately by a chord of the dominant group in the new key.

Samuel Wesley: Psalm chant (?c.1830)

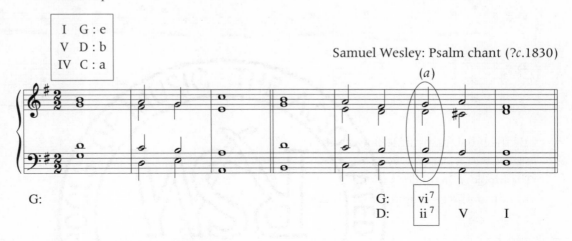

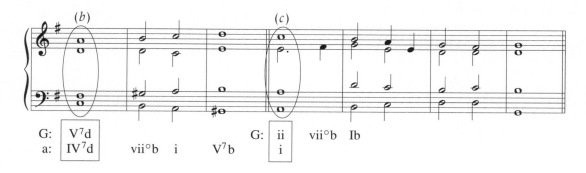

G: V⁷d
a: IV⁷d   vii°b   i   V⁷b

G: ii   vii°b   Ib
i

◆ The circled chords in these examples are the pivot chords, occurring just before V and vii°b.

(a) vi⁷ in the key of G
    = ii⁷ in the new key of D;
    it then moves to V.

(b) V⁷d in the key of G
    = IV⁷d in the new key of A minor;
    V⁷d would be expected to resolve to Ib in G. Instead, the tenor line ascends to G♯, in the melodic scale of A minor, forming chord vii°b in the new key. Notice the difference the G♯ makes.

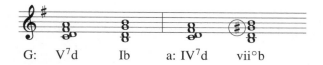

G: V⁷d   Ib   a: IV⁷d   vii°b

(c) i in the key of A minor
    = ii in the home key of G;
    it then moves to vii°b.

In the next extract the modulation uses a **pivot note** (circled), which then forms part of V⁷d of the new key.

Beethoven: Piano Sonata in C minor, Op. 10 No. 1 (c.1795)

(*a*)   the 3rd of the tonic chord of C minor
        = the root of the dominant chord of A♭

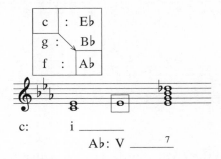

- In an **abrupt** modulation, a chord of the destination key's dominant group appears with no intervening pivot.
- Abrupt modulations are frequently made by a note rising by a semitone in the bass, becoming a new leading note (marked * in the following example). Chord vi⁷b is altered into VI⁷b and can therefore be V⁷b of the new key of F minor.

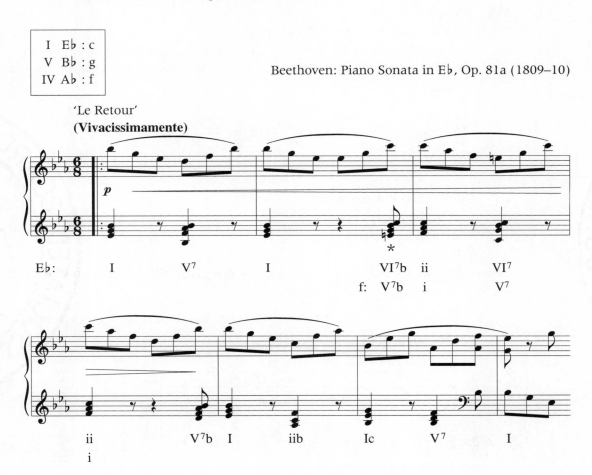

Beethoven: Piano Sonata in E♭, Op. 81a (1809–10)

Phrase modulation

In many hymns, psalm chants and chorales you will find **phrase modulation**. This is where a key is changed for a particular phrase only. A subsequent phrase may revert abruptly to the original key or to another related key. Consider the following examples:

Bach: Chorale

Exercises

121

Identify the modulations in the following chorale. Label the start of the new keys.

Before embarking on the exercise:

1 remind yourself of the related keys;

2 look out for new accidentals.

Bach: Chorale

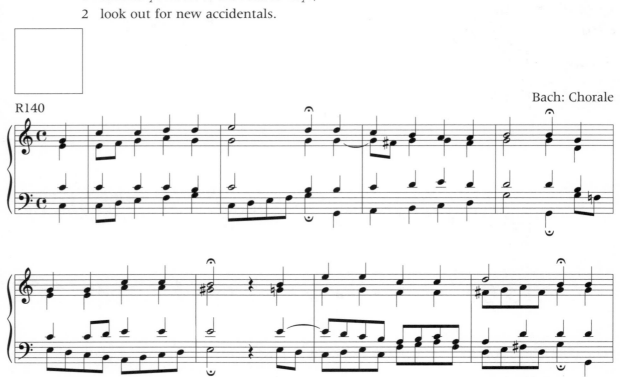

122

Harmonize the following phrases for SATB.

1 Work out the related keys.
2 Sing both the melody and bass lines to find any modulations.
3 Label the chords.
4 Use the figured bass to give you all the information you need, including the new accidentals.

Croft: 'St Anne' (1708)

R106

Bach: Chorale

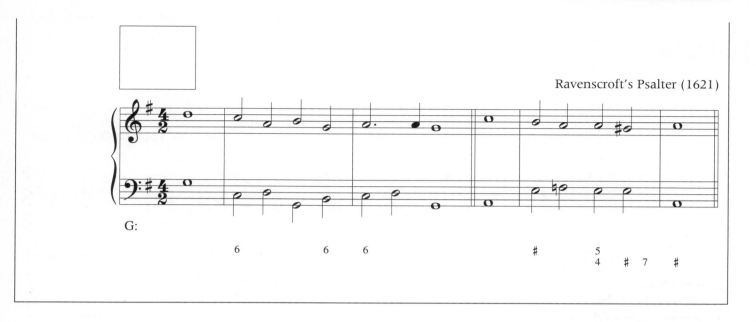

Ravenscroft's Psalter (1621)

'Walking' through keys – when is a modulation not a modulation?

Modulation may represent a decisive shift in key, confirmed by a firm cadence or an extended period in the new key. Sometimes, though, a modulation may be brief, its purpose less to establish a new key than to strengthen a chord in the initial key by a colourful chromatic movement of lines.

Listen to, or play, these bars from Tchaikovsky's *Album for the Young*.

Tchaikovsky: 'Morning Prayer', from *Album for the Young*, Op. 39 No. 1 (1878)

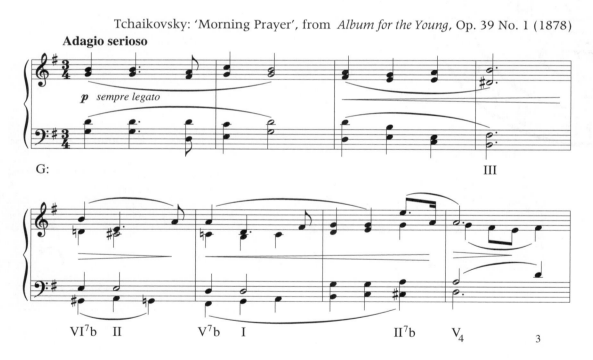

◆ In this case the accidentals may indicate an **altered chord** within the original key rather than a true modulation, and it should be labelled as such. (For 'altered chords', *see* Part 5, Chapter 15.)

◆ It is sometimes difficult to decide whether a modulation has actually taken place if there is no confirming cadence. Much will depend on the speed of the passage and what musical weight is given to the chords in question. There may also be a subjective reaction, since people hear progressions in different ways.

Exercise 123   Label the keys in this excerpt from Schubert.

I	c♯ : E
V	g♯ : B
IV	f♯ : A

Schubert: 'Wanderer' Fantasy, Op. 15 (1822)

- In *Exercise 123* the music is moving slowly enough for the listener to appreciate the brief modulation to F♯ minor (marked *). The move from chord i in C♯ minor to C♯^{7} major (V^7 of F♯ minor) makes a prominent cadence to chord i in F♯ minor, which becomes the most important chord of the phrase.
- Such transitory 'modulations' also occur in passing $^6_3$ and $^6_4$ progressions, sometimes involving chord ii.

Exercise 124   Label this modulation, including the chords involved.

I	C : a
V	G : e
IV	F : d

Schumann: *Arabeske*, Op. 18 (1839)

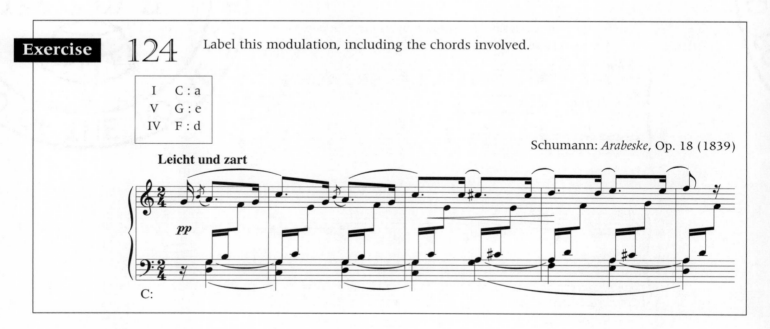

Modulation and the sequence

We saw in Chapter 9 (page 137) that modulations can occur in conjunction with sequences and the progression of 5ths, and we noted two examples by Bach. These modulations are identified by the new accidentals, as we have seen.

- Sequential modulations may 'lift' or 'point' the phrase with colour and interest. In the following extract note:
  - at (*a*) the effect of the modulation to A minor, using vii^{d7} at the climax of the musical line, followed by V^7, with a phrase that is repeated in a sequence in G minor;
  - at (*b*) the way Bach modifies the A minor chord of the previous bar by introducing the E♭ to create a pivot chord into G minor.

J. S. Bach: Praeludium, from *Little Notebook for W. F. Bach* (1720)

Exercises **125** Identify the modulations in the following extract. Play it through.

Beethoven: Symphony No. 7 in A, Op. 92 (1812)

126   Here now is an exercise to practise the work you have done on modulations.
1   Complete for SATB these simple chorale phrases, which include modulations.
2   Work out the related keys and write them in the boxes provided.
3   Sing both the melody and bass lines to find any modulations.
4   Label the chords.

Bach: Chorales

Musical structure or form

We have suggested that the musical forms of the tonal period depended on key contrast, on modulation **away from** and **back to** the tonic. *Exercise 127* demonstrates this importance with some movements in so-called **binary form**.

◆ You will notice that each is in two sections, the second longer than the first.

◆ The opening and closing bars of each section may be very similar.

◆ The first section closes either **on** the dominant chord (an imperfect cadence), or **in** the dominant key (or in the relative major, if the piece is in a minor key). The modulations create contrast and colour.

◆ There may be further key changes in the first part of the second section B to C minor.

◆ There will usually be a return to the opening material and the tonic key in the latter bars of the second section.

Exercise 127   Play or listen to these pieces. Note the related keys in the boxes provided before you start work on the questions.

1   Label the sections A and B.

2   Indicate the modulations.

3   Label the harmony at the cadence points. These are normally at two- or four-bar intervals.

4   Indicate the point of return to the A material in the B section if it occurs.

5   Bracket any sequences and note any recurring melodic and rhythmic phrases.

Bach: Orchestral Suite No. 2 in B minor (*c*.1738)
arranged for keyboard by Bach

Polonaise

Purcell: 'Fairest Isle', from *King Arthur* (1691)

Bb:

Stölzel: *Little Notebook for W. F. Bach* (1720)

Menuet

g:

Modulation to 'Remote' Keys

CHAPTER 13

Throughout the tonal period modulations to remote keys were used for expressive purposes. Even in nineteenth-century repertory, where they are quite common, they can still surprise. Composers expected their performers to convey these musical surprises as effectively as possible by the subtle use of timing or dynamics. The effect of modulations to distant keys depends on the character of the music and on the subjective response of the listener or performer. Some distant modulations may evoke a sense of utter tranquillity, others a profound melancholy and restlessness.

Remote modulations in fast tempi may create comic or witty effects. There are many examples in the music of Stravinsky, Prokofiev and the group of French composers known as 'Les Six'.

Examples of remote modulation fall into various groups. We shall look briefly at these in this chapter.

Modulation from tonic minor to major or vice versa

◆ The change of colour makes this type of modulation highly effective.

This example is from the start of the last verse of 'Gute Nacht' from Schubert's desolate song cycle *Die Winterreise*. The unexpected key change to D major creates a brief respite from the otherwise D minor tonality.

Schubert: 'Gute Nacht', from *Die Winterreise* (1828)

The change of key colour is also evident in this extract from this sonata movement by Mozart.

Exercise 128   Bracket the key changes.

I   a : C
V   e : G
IV d : F

Mozart: Piano Sonata in A minor, K310 (1778)

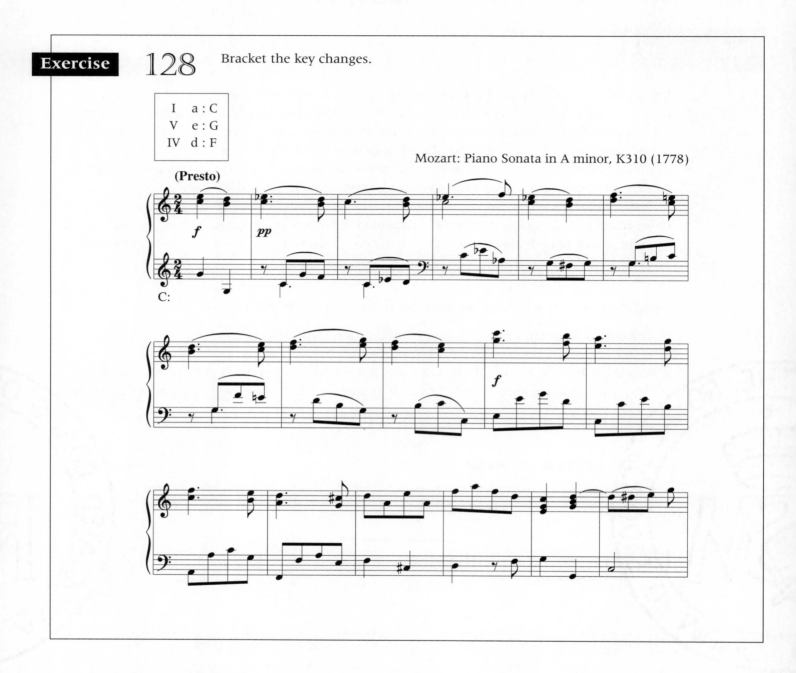

◆ Such a move sometimes becomes the starting point for further modulation.

In his piano Fantasia K475, for example, Mozart uses the move from F major to F minor to open up a wider range of keys through which he can modulate. This decorated sequence takes the music into the remote key of E♭ minor. Play or listen to this passage.

Mozart: Fantasia in C minor, K475 (1785)

Remote modulation using a pivot note

No matter how distant from each other, two keys will always share some notes that can act as a modulating link between them. Such a move is always highly effective because the listener is often caught unawares.

Exercise 129 In the following extract, notice the movement from B major to G major at bars 8–9, using the note B as a link. Play or listen to this extract, and note the **expressive** effect of the modulation. Label the harmony to see how Beethoven achieves it.

I E : c♯
V B : g♯
IV A : f♯

Beethoven: Piano Concerto No. 3 in C minor, Op. 37 (*c.*1800)

G: vi

e: i   V⁷   VI   E: aug. 6 (It.)   V

In the first movement of his great String Quintet in C major, Schubert moves to E♭ for the second subject. The surprise is all the greater because he at first very emphatically reaches the chord of G major, and then slides down to E♭ and a lilting Viennese excursion. The long-held G acts as a pivot note between the chords of G major and E♭.

Schubert: String Quintet in C, D956, Op. 163 (1828)

Elgar uses the same technique in the *Enigma Variations*, in the join between variations 8 and 9 ('Nimrod').

Elgar: *Variations on an Original Theme (Enigma)*, Op. 36 (1899)

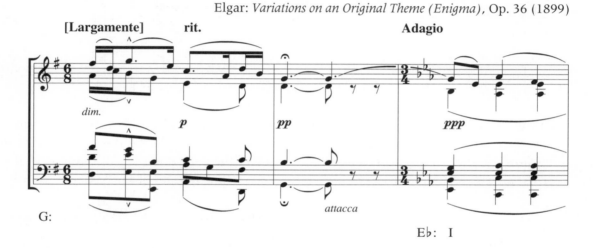

Remote modulation using a pivot chord

A chromatic or tonally ambiguous chord, i.e. one that does not belong definitively to a key or 'family' of keys, can be used to move to a remote key. The **diminished 7th** and **augmented 6th chords**, for example, can be used. (For the diminished 7th, *see* Chapter 6, p. 79; for the augmented 6th, *see* Chapter 15, p. 243.)

In bar 11 of the Beethoven extract above, for example, notice how the C major chord (VI in E minor) is made into an augmented 6th chord leading to a B major chord (V) before returning to E major (I).

The sound of the diminished 7th chord permeates the harmony in Bach's Fantasia and Fugue in G minor. It is characteristically used as an expressive substitute for V[7] to modulate to remote keys. In the following example, notice the **ambiguous** nature of vii[d7], where by **suggesting**, not writing, an **enharmonic change**, i.e. the B♭ to an A♯, Bach moves swiftly from D minor to B minor (marked *).

Bach: Fantasia and Fugue in G minor for organ, BWV 542

In the following extract, from Liszt's transcription for piano of Bach's work, the harmony is also decorated with suspensions. Notice the enharmonic change which stops the music from moving towards the sharper keys (F♯) and brings it back to the related flat key of C minor. Notice also the cross- or false relation (G♯–G♮) at (*a*) which increases the tension of the passage.

Bach, transcribed Liszt: Fantasia and Fugue in G minor

Remote modulations via the dominant 7th

◆ The dominant 7th and its related 'family' chords enable the music to move suddenly into unrelated keys, because the V$^{(7)}$–I progression is so strong and unequivocal.

In the opening bars of the overture to *Hansel and Gretel*, notice the modulation to E♭ (boxed). It has moved away unexpectedly from C major and D minor, and starts a modulating sequence. Notice also how the dynamic marking ⟨ *p* will 'point' this modulation in performance.

Exercise

130 Label the modulations in the brackets.

I	C : a
V	G : e
IV	F : d

Humperdinck: Prelude to *Hansel and Gretel* (1893)

Remote modulation by chromatic movement and sequences

◆ The most chromatic harmony may stretch to the limit the listener's ability to distinguish a key centre.

In another example from his Fantasia, Mozart uses a modulating sequence which descends by semitones in the bass. However, the dominant 7th **chords** suggested never resolve, although the dominant 7th **notes** do (except in bars 1–2 of the example below), and the music creates a sense of unease, as if it is in 'limbo'. It is one of the strangest passages of harmony Mozart ever wrote.

Mozart: Fantasia in C minor, K475 (1785)

In the following passage from Act 3 of Wagner's *Siegfried* there is also a modulating sequence in which the bass descends chromatically. The same restless quality as in the Mozart is this time evoked by diminished 7ths moving on to dominant 7ths which never resolve.

Wagner: *Siegfried*, Act 3 (1857)

Even though it is highly chromatic, the passage is very strong because of:
- the presence of pivot notes;
- the bass line that moves from dominant to tonic in bars 1–2 and 4–5;
- the descending bass line that supports the rising sequential melody.

◆ In both the previous passages our awareness of key or tonal centre is suspended. That is rather rare in Mozart's music, but common in Wagner's from seventy years or so later.

Remote modulation without warning

Composers may abandon any standard method of modulating, and instead simply **leap** to a new key. Such moments are often accompanied by an abrupt change of dynamic, texture or register.

We saw in Chapter 12, page 169 an example by Haydn. In fact, he often moves into an unrelated key to surprise his listener with a touch of drama or good humour. In the next example notice the sudden change of dynamic and register, and the sense of expectation created by the pause.

Haydn: Piano Sonata in E♭, Hob XVI/52 (1794)

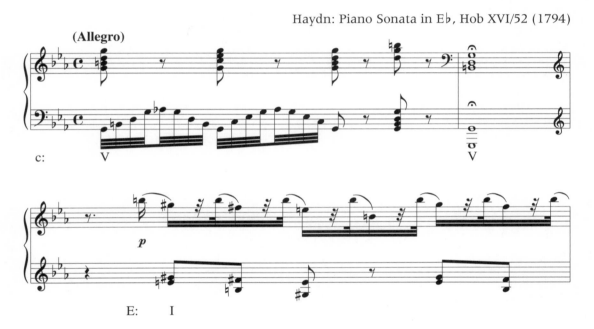

Key changes between movements

In the Baroque and early Classical periods, separate movements of the same work were usually in the same key or in closely related keys. From the end of the eighteenth century, however, this changed, and there are many examples of effective, distant key changes **between** movements in a work.

In his Third Piano Concerto (c.1800), Beethoven moves from the opening movement's C minor to the serene key of E major for the second movement (a). Perhaps he knew Haydn's String Quartet, Op. 76 No. 5 (c.1797), which moves from D major in the first movement to the very unusual key of F♯ major for the second (b).

(a) Beethoven   (b) Haydn

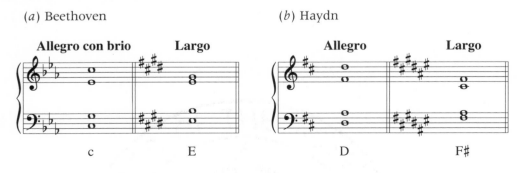

MELODIC AND HARMONIC DECORATION

Introduction to Part 5

Since music has the power to move us (to 'strike the heart', as the text for Purcell's 1692 Ode for St Cecilia's Day, *Hail! Bright Cecilia!*, has it), it becomes clear that composers have developed an appropriate musical language to do this and to communicate the emotions. Our awareness of this language of expression will help us to be more sensitive performers and listeners.

Composers in the Baroque period established general practices in composition which now we tend to take for granted. These practices originated in word-setting, but came to apply to all music, including instrumental.

There were two broad conventions:

1 Music expressing joyful or optimistic emotions (or 'affections') would normally be fast-moving and diatonic, written in a major key, with predominantly rising melodic lines. If the music was orchestral, the higher registers and bright-sounding instruments would also be used.

   This extract from Purcell's semi-opera *The Fairy Queen* (1692) illustrates these points:
   - it is in a major key;
   - it has a brisk tempo;
   - there is a trumpet obbligato with fanfare-like melody lines, imitated by the voice (compare bars 1–2 with 5–6);
   - it features exuberant ascending diatonic figurations.

Purcell: 'Hark! hark! the ech'ing air a triumph sings', from *The Fairy Queen* (1692)

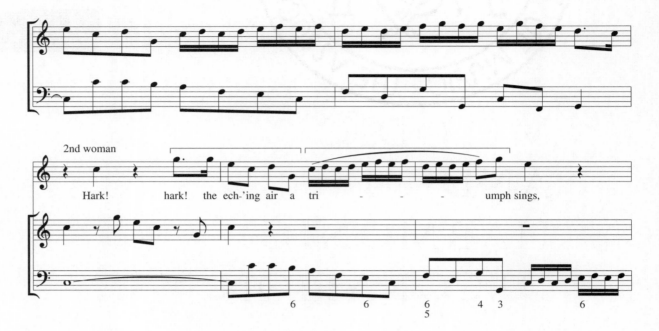

2   In contrast, music expressing sorrow, tension and despair would normally be written in a slow tempo, in a minor key, with descending melodic lines, and might characteristically feature dissonance and chromaticism. The textures and sounds often reflected the subdued nature of the composition, with lower registers and lyrical instrumentation.

     In this recitative from the 1692 Ode for St Cecilia's Day, *Hail! Bright Cecilia!*, Purcell shows how appropriate music sets off the meaning of the words. Notice:

- the change of chord from major to minor on 'and straight we grieve';
- the use of the diminished 7th (vii^{d7}) to 'paint' the word 'grieve';
- the tortuous melody line, decorated with chromatic alterations and suspensions;
- the gradually descending lines;
- the repetition of 'and straight we grieve' at a lower pitch.

Purcell: Ode, *Hail! Bright Cecilia!* (1692)

Melodic and harmonic decoration are intrinsic to all tonal music as a means of expressive communication. This final part of *Harmony in Practice* will consider the whole area, including the vital elements of dissonant decoration and chromatic writing.

Melodic Decoration

CHAPTER 14

Decoration has always been a powerful, expressive force in the visual arts, whether in the intricacies of a medieval stained-glass window, a seventeenth-century French tapestry or in the paintings of the great masters.

One of the oldest techniques in musical composition is the decoration of a melodic line with non-harmony notes. Such decoration forms the basis of writing variations, and there are numerous examples from before the tonal era of variations for virginals and lutes. The following example is typical of the style, in which the few melody notes are enriched with many more. The circled notes of the decorated version show the melodic line. These are in addition to the **ornaments** (♪).

Byrd: *Pavana Lachrymae*, from the Fitzwilliam Virginal Book (*c.*1619)

(repeat – decorated)

The name of the Baroque era is synonymous with ornate decoration, and composers in that period incorporated the technique of embellishment into every aspect of composition and in every form. Vocal and instrumental lines alike abounded in elaborate figurations, which were exhilarating in fast tempi and expressive in slow. The difference from the earlier period was that the line became more directed and in the slower writing was more dissonant. Here are two examples from Bach's Italian Concerto.

Bach: Italian Concerto, 3rd movt (1735)

Bach: Italian Concerto, 2nd movt (1735)

Performers in this period were expected to be able to improvise a decorated melody line in slow movements, especially when a section came to be repeated. Thus two performances would never be exactly the same. The following example is from the slow movement of Corelli's Violin Sonata, Op. 5 No. 3. It shows the original violin line and a highly decorated version. It was published in Amsterdam around 1715 by Pierre Mortier, who claimed that the ornaments (or 'graces') were 'comme il les joue' ('as he [Corelli] plays them').

Corelli: Violin Sonata, Op. 5 No. 3 (pub. 1715)

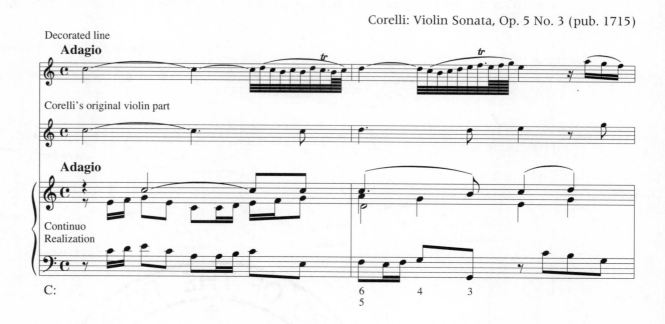

The same principles were retained during the later Classical and Romantic periods, although the supporting harmonies, as well as the melodic lines, became more chromatic. The embroidery of a melodic line with graceful arabesques was regarded as especially expressive in slow movements, the dissonance serving only to increase the emotional effect.

Mozart: Piano Concerto No. 23 in A, K488 (1786)

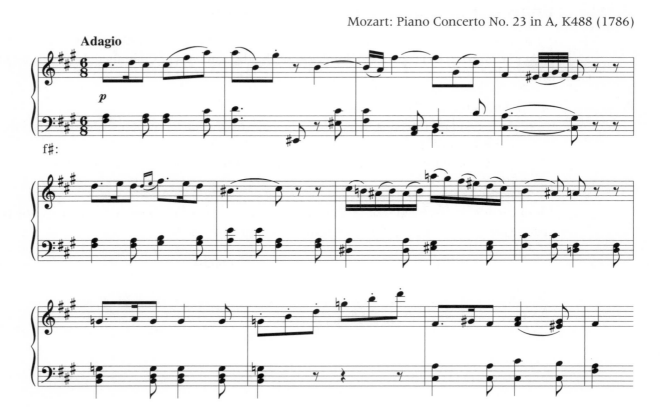

In the nineteenth century, virtuoso music was characterized by rapid figuration, and fast-moving and often highly chromatic harmony which modulated freely.

Chopin: Prelude in B♭ minor, Op. 28 No. 16 (1836–9)

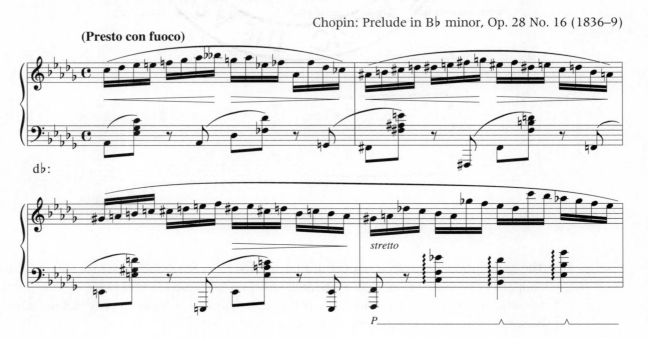

Understanding decoration and dissonance

Let us now look at the different forms of melodic decoration and how composers have used them. The table on page 203 provides a summary of the decorative types, numbered as they are discussed below.

Decoration notes may be consonant or dissonant:
- the consonant intervals, which usually make up the harmony notes, are major and minor 3rds and 6ths, and the perfect octaves and 5ths (from the bass);
- the dissonant intervals, which make up the **non-harmony notes**, are 2nds, 4ths, 7ths and 9ths.

These categories were more or less established by the time the English composer John Dunstable died in 1453, and remained in place throughout the tonal period.

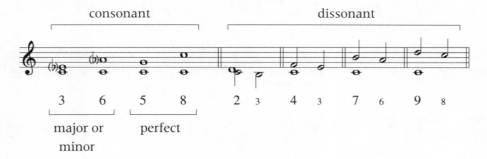

Note that the intervals which are dissonant with respect to the bass notes create varying degrees of tension or instability. The sense of expectancy that results in the mind of the listener is satisfied when the unstable interval resolves, usually downwards to one more stable (we shall examine this further later in the chapter).
- Dissonances in melody lines in the texture are either accented or unaccented, according to their position in relation to the beat. The most effective dissonances are accented.
- Dissonances are also either prepared (the suspension) or unprepared.
- Dissonances may be altered chromatically.

Table of decoration notes

Consonant decoration

1   harmony note
2   subsidiary or auxiliary note

Dissonant and unprepared decoration

3   unaccented passing note
4   accented passing note
5   unaccented auxiliary note (upper and lower)
6   accented auxiliary note (upper and lower)
7   cambiata ⎫
8   échappée ⎬ changing notes
9   anticipation note
10 appoggiatura
11 cross- or false relation
12 long passing note

Dissonant and prepared decoration

13 suspension
14 retardation

Several of these decorations may be altered chromatically.

You will find that it is possible to break down passages of elaborate figuration into various types of consonant and dissonant decorations. It is helpful to put them into various categories and to understand their use.

Study all of the examples given in this chapter and memorize the sounds carefully; it is often clearer to make the point with the music rather than with words.

Consonant decoration

1 Harmony note

◆ Harmony notes belong to the chord which is implied or stated in the other parts or the bass line.

2 Subsidiary or auxiliary harmony note

◆ These are notes on unaccented or subsidiary beats that belong to the implied or actual harmony.

In these examples from Book 1 of the *Well-Tempered Clavier*, **all** the notes in both hands are harmony or subsidiary harmony notes.

Bach: Prelude in C, from *The Well-Tempered Clavier*, Bk 1 No. 1 (1722)

Bach: Prelude in D minor, from *The Well-Tempered Clavier*, Bk 1 No. 6 (1722)

In both examples note that the chords change over a tonic pedal note, which may or may not contribute to the harmony.

◆ The Classical 'Alberti' bass pattern included subsidiary harmony notes, which prolonged the sounding of the chord. Some left-hand figurations in nineteenth-century piano music had the same effect, often helped by the sustaining pedal.

Exercise **131** Circle the auxiliary harmony notes in the left-hand part in one bar of each of these examples. You will notice in both pieces that the left hand provides the harmonic framework while the right hand embroiders the melody line with figuration including dissonances.

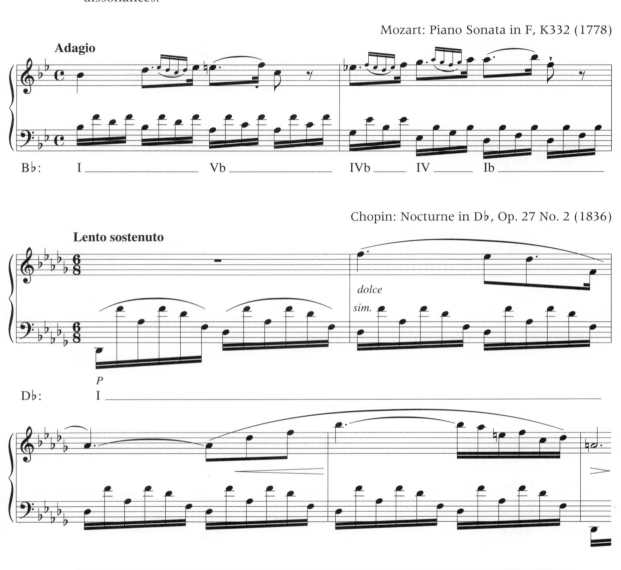

Dissonant and unprepared decoration

3 Unaccented passing note

◆ Passing notes lie between harmony notes, linking them by stepwise movement. The movement of the line can be in any direction and in any part of the texture. An unaccented passing note will fall on a weak beat or part of the beat in the bar.

4 Accented passing note

◆ Accented passing notes have the same function and resolution as unaccented ones, but they fall **on** the beat or on a strong part of the beat. They are a type of appoggiatura, and move by step to a harmony note on a weaker beat or part of the beat.

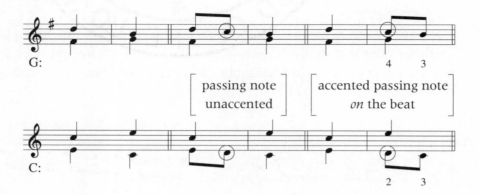

G:

passing note
unaccented

accented passing note
on the beat

C:

Exercises

132

Circle the unaccented passing notes in this passage.

Bach: Two-Part Invention No. 4 in D minor (1723)

d: i _____   vii^{d7}_____   i _____   vii^{d7}____   ib _____   vii^{d7}b _____   i

133

Circle the accented passing notes in this passage.

Bach: Prelude in D, from *The Well-Tempered Clavier*, Bk 1 No. 5 (1722)

D: I _____   Ib ____ I ____   ii ____   vib ___ V⁷ ____ V⁷b   I

5 Unaccented auxiliary note

◆ This is really an ornament, a written-out **mordent**. The main (harmony) note alternates with the note a step above or below. The alternate note appears on a weaker beat or part of the beat. An unaccented auxiliary note can appear in any voice or part.

6 Accented auxiliary note

◆ The auxiliary note this time falls **on** the beat or on the stronger part of the beat. Like the accented passing note, it is a kind of appoggiatura.

unaccented   accented   unaccented   accented
upper auxiliary   upper auxiliary   lower auxiliary   lower auxiliary

d:

Exercise 134   Ring the auxiliary notes (and mark them 'aux.'), accented auxiliary notes ('acc. aux.') and accented passing notes ('a. p. n.') in the following passages by Bach.

Bach: Two-Part Invention No. 8 in F (1723)

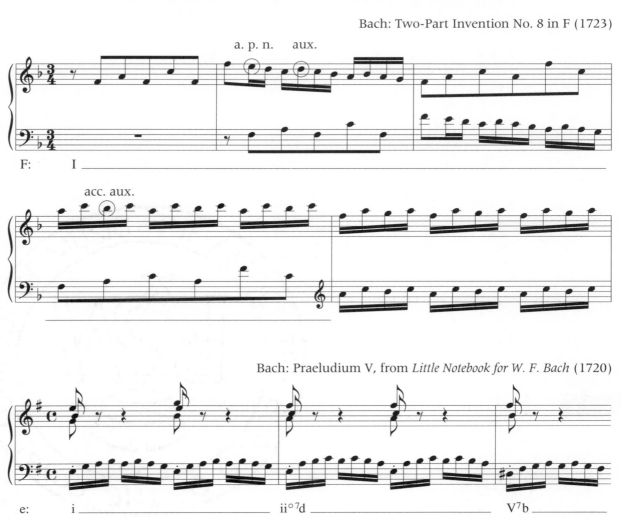

Bach: Praeludium V, from *Little Notebook for W. F. Bach* (1720)

Several patterns of ornament move from dissonant notes by leap rather than by step. They are called **changing notes** and the following are the two most important types.

7 The cambiata

◆ The cambiata (Italian for 'changing' note) is a figure from Renaissance counterpoint. It moves **down** from a consonance by step, followed by a leap, often of a 3rd, in the **same** direction. That note is then left by step in the opposite direction, to a harmony note in the following chord, resolving the 7th.

◆ In music of the Renaissance it became a favourite cadential formula, often combined with a suspension.

Bennet: 'All creatures now are merry minded' (*c.*1601)

C: 4   3

8   *The échappée*

◆ The échappée (French for 'escaped' note) is a figure from Baroque counterpoint; it is also called a changing note. It involves a step up or down from a consonance, followed by a leap in the other direction off a dissonance to a harmony note. The échappée is almost always unaccented.

G: = leap off a 4th   = leap off a 2nd   = leap off a 7th

◆ The échappée often appears in a dotted rhythm, and is common in the music of Lully and Purcell.

Exercise   135   Ring the échappée notes in the following extracts.

Purcell: 'Thus, the ever-grateful Spring', from *The Fairy Queen* (1692)

Bach: Two-Part Invention No. 3 in D (1723)

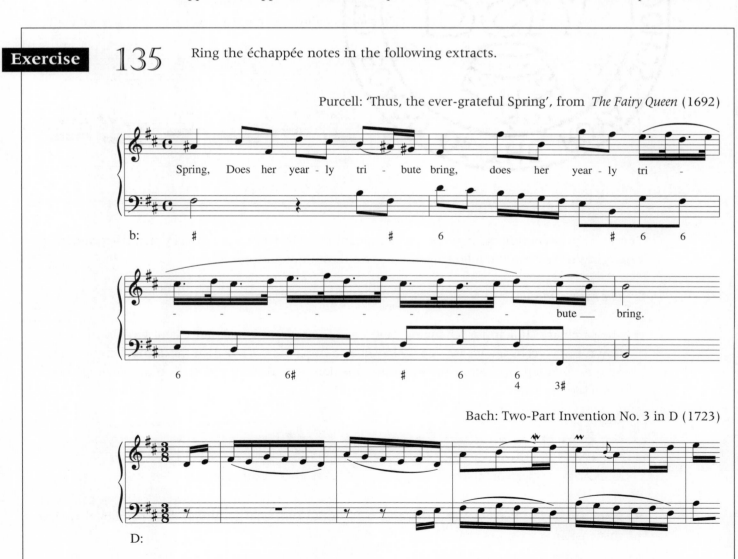

◆ In the Classical period it adds a delicate decoration to the melodic line.

Exercise 136   Ring the échappée notes implied in the melody line in the following extract.

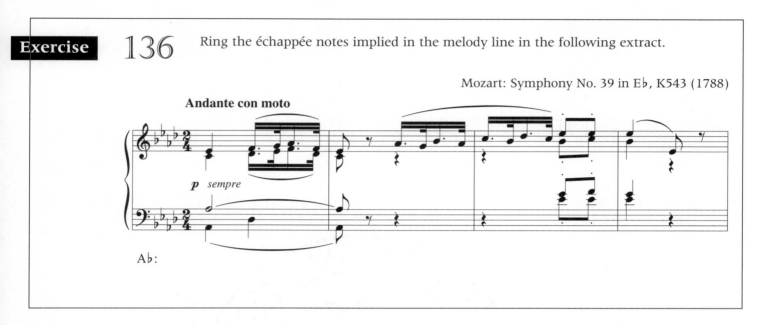

Mozart: Symphony No. 39 in E♭, K543 (1788)

◆ Other patterns of changing notes involve **two** dissonant notes next to each other, for example:

Here is an extract from the Fugue in F major, from Book 1 of Bach's *The Well-Tempered Clavier*, which illustrates such a pattern (circled notes in bar 2):

Bach: Fugue in F, from *The Well-Tempered Clavier*, Bk 1 No. 11 (1722)

This example also shows in the last two notes of the right hand the principle of the **anticipation note**.

9 Anticipation note

◆ This is a telling dissonance, usually found in the melody line at cadences. At a perfect cadence, for example, the tonic is sounded early, against the dominant harmony.
◆ Sometimes notes will be anticipated in two parts simultaneously:

Corelli: Trio Sonata, Op. 1 No. 11 (1683)

The sounding together of the leading note and the tonic, a Baroque trait, is particularly effective in slow tempi:

Corelli: Trio Sonata, Op. 2 No. 1 (1685)

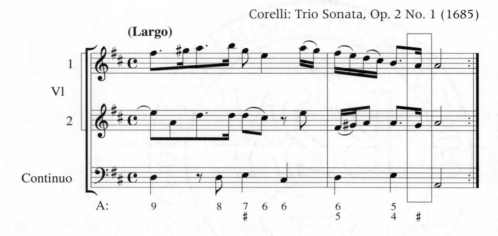

10   The appoggiatura

◆ The appoggiatura (literally 'leaning note') is a dissonant note normally approached by a jump and quitted by a step, up or down, to a consonant note.

◆ Appoggiatura is often used as a collective term for unprepared dissonances on strong beats, including accented passing and auxiliary notes.

◆ It is often the most telling dissonance; the wider the approaching jump and the longer the dissonance lasts, the more expressive the effect.

Exercise 137   The appoggiaturas in these phrases from Mozart's Piano Sonata in B♭, K333 are typical of the style. Ring the appoggiaturas and notice the dissonances they create.

Mozart: Piano Sonata in B♭, K333, 2nd movt (1778)

Chromatic alterations

All the dissonances discussed so far can themselves be decorated by altering notes chromatically. The semitone movement can create more subtle and expressive effects.

Listen to the sound of this example:

Bach: Suite in G minor for Lute, BWV 995 (1727–31)

Note that the accidentals being introduced are not acting as leading notes in a modulation.

Exercise **138**   The following excerpts are characteristic of the expressive melodic decoration used during the Classical period.

Play them through and circle the chromatic and diatonic appoggiaturas.

Label the harmony. (Remember that the harmony note will follow the appoggiatura, which is a decoration.)

◆ As the nineteenth century progressed, appoggiaturas became a prominent feature.

Exercises   139   In this example, from Schumann's song cycle *Dichterliebe*, notice the important position of appoggiaturas in the melody and the poignant effect they create.

     Circle any other appoggiaturas and continue labelling the harmonies by reducing the texture to chords on one stave, as shown in the first two lines.

Schumann: 'Im wunderschönen Monat Mai', from *Dichterliebe*, Op. 48 (1840)

al - le Knos - pen spran - gen   da ist   in mei - nem
all   the buds _ were blow - ing,   I felt   with - in   my

Her - zen   die Lie - be auf   ge - gan - gen.
heart, ____   The flow'r   of love   was grow - ing.

rit.

140   Identify the appoggiaturas in these two examples by Brahms, and note the considerable effect they have on the harmony. In the second piece some chords are decorated with two and even three dissonances, giving **double** and **triple appoggiaturas**.

◆ Chromatic appoggiaturas became so widely used in the nineteenth century that the sense of key sometimes became 'blurred' or lost altogether. The whole tonal system was weakened, with the result that composers like Debussy and Schoenberg sought to develop other methods of composition.

11   Cross-relations

◆ We looked at the cross-relation (sometimes known as 'false' relation) in Chapter 4. It arises from the juxtaposition or sounding together of the sharpened and flattened leading note or 7th. It was originally characteristic of English Renaissance music, where it was often associated with 'word-painting', but it was used as an expressive dissonance throughout the tonal period.

Exercise 141   Identify the cross-relations in the following extracts. Label all the other circled dissonances.

C. P. E. Bach: Sonata in B minor (1779)

Mozart: Piano Sonata in B♭, K282 (1774)

Mozart: 'Lacrymosa', from *Requiem* (1791)

12   Long passing note

◆ Long passing notes 'walking throough' static chords create dissonance and hence tension in the music.

Exercise 142 Here is an extract from the Adagio of Mozart's String Quintet in D, K593. Play this through and listen to the effect of the long passing notes in bars 1 and 5. Figure the dissonances. Ring the double appoggiatura.

Mozart: String Quintet in D, K593 (1790)

13 Dissonant and prepared decoration – the suspension

◆ The suspension is perhaps the most important type of dissonance, with a history that stretches back to the early Renaissance. Its characteristic sound can be heard in part-writing in practically all tonal music.

In the Renaissance dissonances were treated quite strictly. The suspension was the only dissonance permitted on a strong beat (passing notes could occur on unaccented beats only) but it had to be prepared. Unprepared dissonances on strong beats made their appearance only in the early Baroque period. Monteverdi, who made effective and original use of all kinds of dissonances in his operas, defended their use in the interests of dramatic expression.

The working of the suspension

In Chapter 5 we looked briefly at the working of the suspension, where it often appears at cadence points. This section gives a wider overview of this important decoration and includes some revision material.

◆ You will remember that there are three steps in the working of the melodic suspension:

1 the dissonance is **prepared** as a consonance on a weak beat;
2 it is **sounded** on a strong beat;
3 it **resolves** (usually downwards, by step) on a subsequent weaker beat.

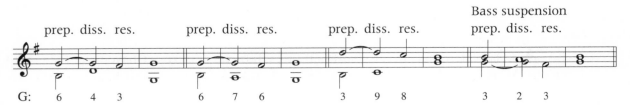

This last example shows the only bass suspension in common use.

◆ Renaissance music was predominantly vocal, and the preparation of a dissonance as a consonance, that is, a harmony note, ensured that it was sung in tune.

◆ The dissonance may be tied (suspended) or sounded.

Exercise 143   Suspensions in two parts show the 'bare bones' of a progression.

Figure the following suspensions. Play and sing them so that you can hear the different intervals.

It is useful to number the minim beats above the music to ensure that the suspension or dissonance sounds on a strong beat, **1** or **3**.

◆ Suspensions often proceed in 'chains', where the note of resolution becomes the preparation for the next dissonance. This repeated sequence is a characteristic feature of the music of Corelli and Vivaldi.

◆ Note that the phrases in brackets are **syncopated**. A tie or syncopation may alert you to the presence of a suspension.

◆ Consecutive octaves may not 'hide' in a suspension (*a*). However, you will find that Bach often uses a suspension to avoid consecutive 5ths (*b*).

Bach: Chorale

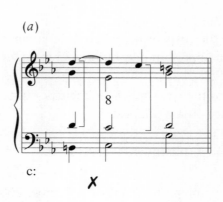

◆ Suspensions may occur in any part, including the bass. As we have seen, though, the only really satisfactory bass suspension occurs when the 3rd of the chord is held over or delayed.

Harmony at the cadence

(*See* Chapter 5)

◆ From the Renaissance period on, the harmony at cadences was decorated with dissonances of some kind, particularly suspensions.
◆ Chord V in a perfect cadence was frequently decorated with a 4–3 suspension and this became one of the strongest and most widely used patterns.

Exercise 144 Realize in four parts the figured bass of these cadential phrases from various chorales. Remember to prepare the dissonance in the same part.

Label the harmony before you add a convincing cadential melody line. Check for consecutives before and after you add the alto and tenor parts.

Bach: Chorales

Further suspension treatment

Composers in the tonal period elaborated basic suspensions in various expressive ways. You will enjoy the sensation of dissonance more if you play or sing the extracts in this section.

◆ The **inversion** may change under the note of resolution:

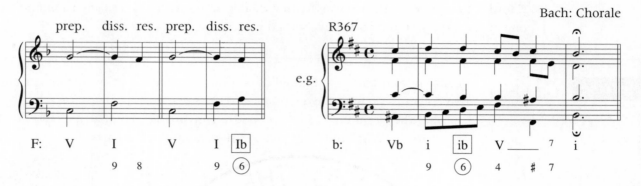

Bach: Chorale

Exercise 145 Figure the suspensions and label the harmony in these examples.

Bach: Chorales

◆ The **chord** may change under the note of resolution:

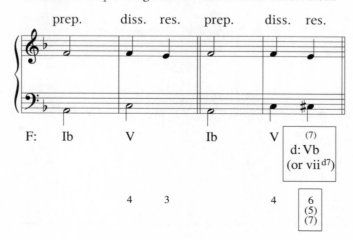

Exercise **146** Identify the chord change with the resolution of the suspension in the following extract by Bach. Label the harmony.

Bach: Chorale

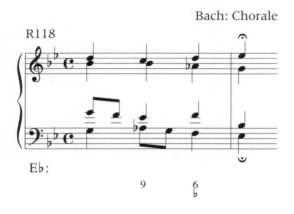

In this extract from a trio sonata by Corelli the chord and even the key change at the end of the second bar (*b*). The extract also shows examples of changing inversions (*a*).

Corelli: Trio Sonata, Op. 2 No. 7 (1685)

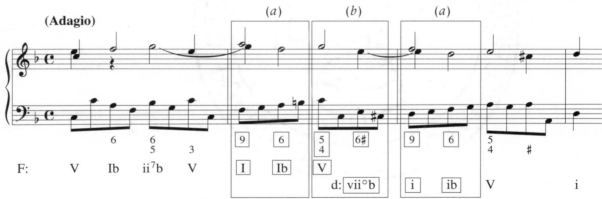

◆ The resolution itself may be decorated. Many of the following patterns were developed by Renaissance composers:

(*a*) the basic pattern;

(*b*) using a lower auxiliary note with an anticipation note;

(*c*) repeating the dissonance;

(*d*) using an anticipation note;

(*e*) using a cambiata (down a 3rd);

(*f*) moving to another note of the chord of resolution.

Here is an extract from a madrigal by Thomas Tomkins:

Tomkins: 'When David heard' (1622)

◆ Later composers added other decorations to the suspension pattern, such as chromatic appoggiaturas, which created more tension.

Exercises 147 Play through this expressive passage and identify and label the various decorations which are circled.

Bach: Fugue in C minor, from *The Well-Tempered Clavier*, Bk 2 No. 2 (1744)

148   The next extract features the progression of 5ths. Ring the sequential melody which Bach decorates with a suspension in a fluid semiquaver figuration. Label the harmony.

Bach: Fugue, from Toccata and Fugue in D minor (*c.*1708)

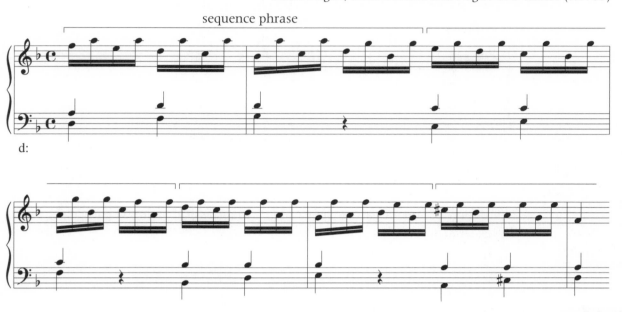

◆ Two or even three notes may be suspended, forming **double** or **triple suspensions**. Figuring the harmony clarifies which dissonances are sounding.

Mozart: Piano Sonata in C, K279 (1775)

Exercise   149   Play through this extract from a prelude by Bach. Circle and figure the suspensions.

Bach: Prelude in F minor, from *The Well-Tempered Clavier*, Bk 2 No. 12 (1744)

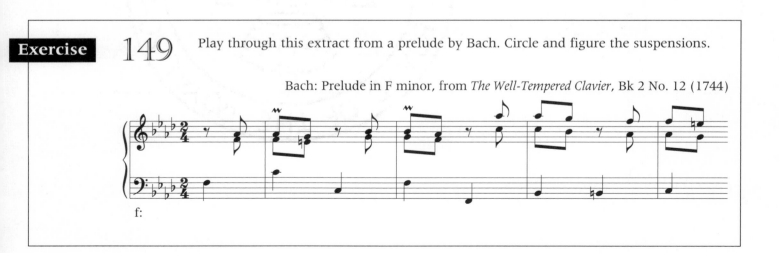

14   *The retardation*

◆ A retardation is a suspension that resolves upwards, usually by a semitone.

Purcell: Verse anthem, 'O Lord of Hosts' (*c*.1682)

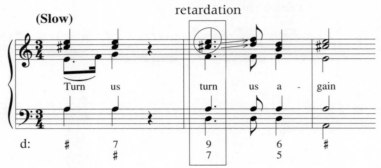

A retardation became a particular feature of the Classical style, when usually two or three notes were suspended.

Exercise   **150**   Identify and figure the retardations in these passages.

Mozart: Piano Sonata in C, K330 (1778)

Mendelssohn: *Song without Words*, Op. 62 No. 3 (1842–4)

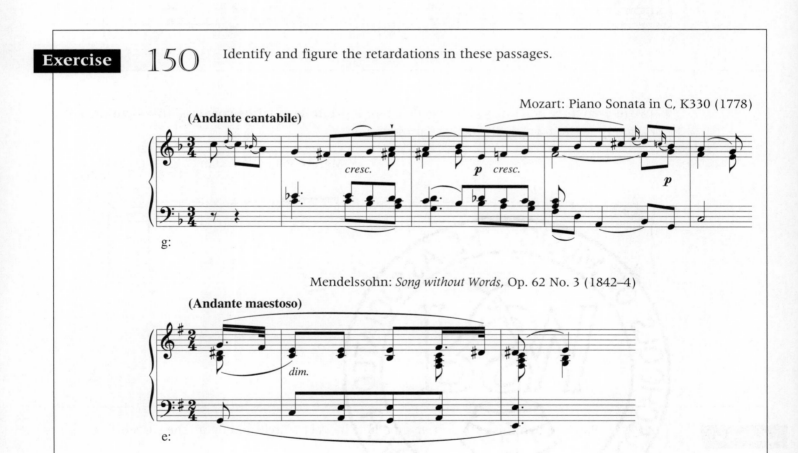

◆ In passages of complex figuration the preparation, dissonance and resolution of suspensions may be hard to find. Other decorating notes may separate them or they may appear in a different octave.

Exercise 151   Ring the dissonances in this extract. Notice the progression of 5ths in the sequential passage with its expressive figuration, as well as the effect of the E♮ accented auxiliary note (marked *) in bars 4–6.

Bach: Prelude in F minor, from *The Well-Tempered Clavier*, Bk 2 No. 12 (1744)

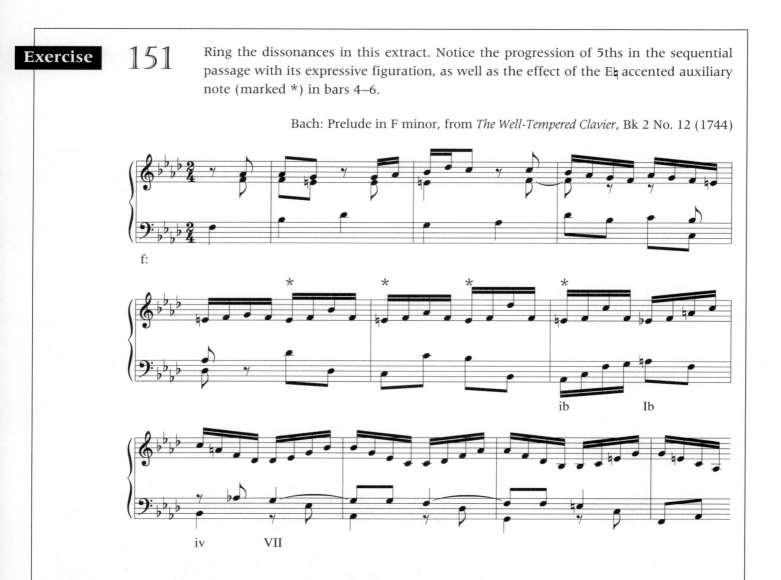

◆ Suspensions were widely used in the tonal era for their expressive effect in slow tempi. In faster music, simple or elaborate suspensions can create drive and forward movement and sometimes great intensity, as in the following example.

Exercises   **152**   Figure the bass line in this extract by Corelli. Notice how the characteristic moving bass line 'underpins' the activity.

Corelli: Concerto Grosso, Op. 6 No. 8, 'Christmas Concerto' (*c*.1680)

153   Circle and figure the accented dissonances in these extracts by Mozart and Chopin. Describe the different kinds of dissonance in the Chopin waltz.

Mozart: Symphony No. 40 in G minor, K550 (1788)

Chopin: Waltz in A♭, Op. 69 No. 1 (*c*.1849)

More elaborate textures

The examples in this book have already shown how elaborate some of Bach's chorale harmonizations can be. His decorations include:

- suspensions;
- auxiliary harmony notes;
- unaccented and accented passing notes;
- auxiliary notes;
- anticipation notes.

Notice that:

- suspensions are commonly held over for only a quaver, so that they can be resolved within the beat; they are frequently sounded and not tied;
- the suspensions often move in chains;
- accented passing notes usually appear on the weaker of the main beats (the second and fourth in common time) in descending lines;
- there are very few appoggiaturas or cambiatas in chorales.

Exercise 154   Identify the circled notes as **either** suspensions (on the strong beats) **or** accented passing notes (the weaker beats).

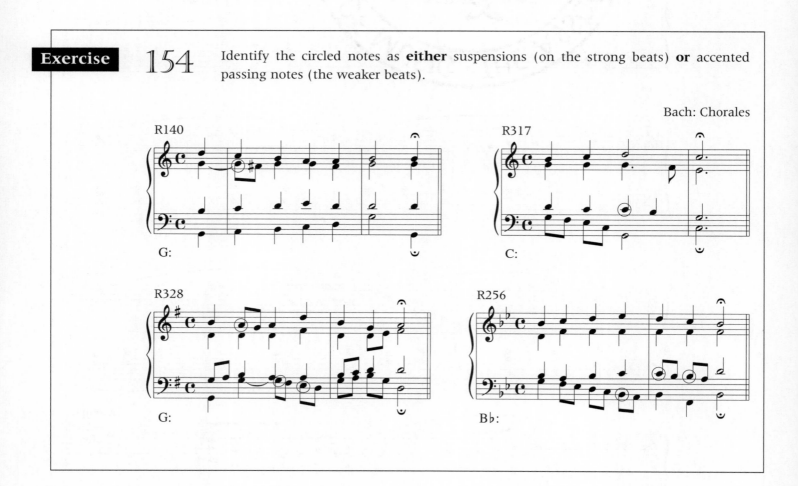

Bach: Chorales

As we saw in Chapter 11, scale movement in the bass part of chorales is always strong and effective. When scales move in quavers there will be some inessential notes, such as auxiliary harmony, accented and unaccented passing notes, auxiliary notes and suspensions. For short passages another part may move parallel with the bass in 3rds or 10ths.

Exercise 155   Identify and label the circled notes in these chorale passages.

Bach: Chorales

Theme and variations

Composers often used melodic embroidery in their **variation** writing. The following extracts by Haydn show the original theme and its first variation.

Haydn: String Quartet in C, Op. 76 No. 3 (1797)

Summary

The wide variety of melodic embellishment that we have looked at in this chapter can be found throughout the tonal period. Some types are associated more with certain periods than with others. The appoggiatura, for instance, is most characteristic of the later eighteenth and nineteenth centuries, often in a chromatically altered form. Throughout the repertory, however, dissonances and their resolution are used to add dynamism and expression to music.

Exercise 156 As a final exercise, consider the following harpsichord piece by Purcell. It first appeared in a vocal version as the air 'Here the deities approve' in the Ode for St Cecilia's Day in 1683, *Welcome to All the Pleasures*. The piece is structured over a chromatic ground bass, and the elaborate melody contains many decorating notes as well as specific ornaments. Suspensions appear in both the melody and the accompaniment.

Play this piece through and identify the circled notes.

The first appearance of the ground bass is bracketed. Bracket all the others.

Purcell: *A New Ground* (1683)

Harmonic Decoration

We find examples of harmonic decoration in the earliest pieces of tonal music from the seventeenth century, and increasingly after that. Like melodic decoration it was considered to enhance musical expression.

The various ways in which harmony is decorated are easy to understand, since they are mostly based on the tonal principles of the Baroque and Classical periods: that is, the music is in a key, and it is based on triads that function in recognizable progressions. In the later part of the nineteenth century, however, the harmony became more complex and difficult to describe.

The principal methods of harmonic decoration are:
- notes in a triad may be altered chromatically to give **altered chords**;
- basic triads may be **extended** by superimposing 3rds to make 7ths, 9ths, 11ths and 13ths;
- the basic diatonic movement of the melodic parts or voices may be decorated chromatically.

We shall see how decorations were used by looking at each of these areas. There are some highly expressive examples in which the melody line is chromatically altered and the triads are extended and altered.

'Extended roman' labelling

The roman labelling that we have used throughout the book to indicate and describe chords can be extended to account for the more chromatic or coloured chords.

Labelling chords:
- helps to develop your aural memory and perception, since the label reflects the **sound** of the chords;
- enables you to identify chords in their functional context;
- draws attention to the **effect** of a chord in its musical context. It is important that this is not overlooked in performances or in your listening.

'Extended roman' labelling clarifies:
- the character of a chord (major, minor, diminished or augmented);
- its inversion (root, first, second or third inversion);
- its extensions (7ths, 9ths, 11ths, 13ths, e.g. V^7, V^9, V^{11}, V^{13});
- its function in the key – I, V, ii, and so on;
- the chromatic inflections that decorate it ($\sharp$, $\flat$ or $\natural$).

Highly chromatic music is sometimes difficult to label because the key or tonality is often lost. The guidelines for labelling are set out on pages xiv–xv. We will look below at how they are applied.

Altered and borrowed chords

◆ Altered chords include chromatically altered notes, other than those in the melodic minor scale.

◆ In the following example (*a*), chord $II^{(7)}$ is an altered chord, because the F$\sharp$ is a chromatic note in C major.

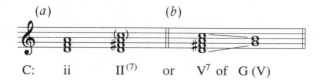

C: ii   II⁽⁷⁾   or   V⁷ of G (V)

◆ Altered chords sometimes behave as **secondary dominants**. In example (*b*) above, II⁷ may also be interpreted as V⁷ of V.

◆ Chords which belong to the minor version of the key, but are chromatic when used in the major, are sometimes called **borrowed chords**. Chords from the major key used in the minor are likewise 'borrowed'. For example, chord iv in E minor is a chromatic chord in E major because it contains a C♮.

Mendelssohn: Overture, *A Midsummer Night's Dream* (1828)

◆ The altered chord will normally occupy the same place in a progression as its diatonic version. The semitone modification in an altered chord creates a stronger progression towards the chord that follows.

Mozart: Piano Concerto No. 24 in C minor, K491 (1786)

◆ The altered notes in a chord are not usually doubled when working out a harmonization. They usually imply strong semitone movement and doubling would almost certainly result in consecutive octaves.

Exercises   **157**   The following exercises will help you to hear and recognize altered chords in different keys. In each case play the tonic triad first. Then:

1 sing the notes of the basic triad without its chromatic alteration;

2 sing the triad, including the chromatic notes.

Use the keyboard to help you if necessary.

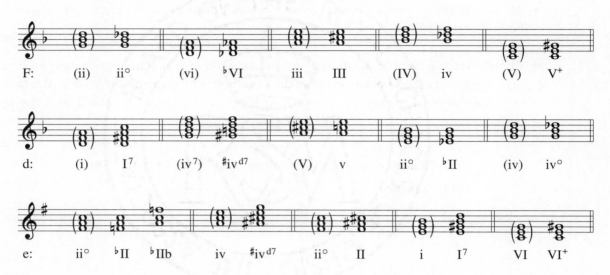

F: (ii)   ii°   (vi)   ♭VI   iii   III   (IV)   iv   (V)   V⁺

d: (i)   I⁷   (iv⁷)   ♯iv ᵈ⁷   (V)   v   ii°   ♭II   (iv)   iv°

e: ii°   ♭II   ♭IIb   iv   ♯iv ᵈ⁷   ii°   II   i   I⁷   VI   VI⁺

158   Sing the following triads and chords, then label them, taking care that your label matches the sound.

G: b:

A♭:   f♯:

E: g:

159   Write down and label some of the possible altered versions of each triad in C major.
Practise singing each triad; always work out the chord from the tonic triad.

C: I$^{(7)}$ I$^{\flat 7}$(V^7 of IV)   i$^{\flat 7}$ I$^+$ $^\sharp$i^{d7}(vii^{d7} of ii)

C: ii$^{(7)}$ ii$^{\circ 7}$ ii^{d7} II^7(V^7 of V) $^\sharp$ii^{d7} (vii^{d7} of iii) $^\flat$II $^\flat$IIb or N^6 aug. 6 (Fr.) $\frac{6\sharp}{4}$ $_3$

C: iii

C: IV   aug. 6 (It.) $\frac{6\sharp}{3}$ aug. 6 (Ger.) $\frac{6\sharp}{5}$ $_3$

C: V

C: vi

C: vii$^{\circ}$

To identify extended chords, especially in a complex texture, you will find it helpful to reduce them to their simplest arrangement of triad or extended triad.

Exercise 160   Identify the altered chords in these passages. Always work from the original triad in the key; the altered notes are easily identified and a modified label applied, which reflects the sound.

Beethoven: String Quartet in D, Op. 18 No. 3 (1798–1800)

Bach: Chorale

Berlioz: Chorus, 'Thou didst leave thy lowly dwelling', from *The Childhood of Christ* (1850–54)

The Neapolitan 6th (♭IIb) chord

◆ The **Neapolitan 6th** is a first inversion triad built on the flattened supertonic. It was so named after Alessandro Scarlatti (1660–1725), an opera composer from Naples, who was known for making great use – too much use in fact – of the chord's expressive qualities. In more discriminating hands the flattened supertonic chord became one of the most effective chromatic chords of the eighteenth and nineteenth centuries.

◆ The Neapolitan 6th is normally found in a minor key, where only the root note needs to be altered. (In a major key two notes would need to be altered.) Its major quality serves to highlight the pathos of the minor key and to enhance the expressiveness of the melody line.

Bach: 'Agnus Dei', from Mass in B minor (*c*.1747–9)

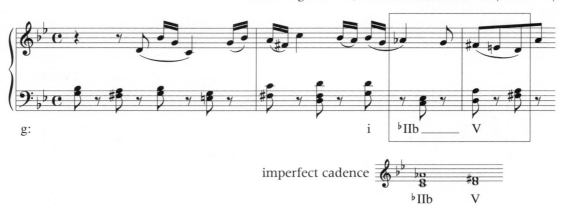

♦ The Neapolitan 6th heightens the intensity of a musical phrase. Listen to the orchestral ritor-nellos in the first and third movements of Mozart's D minor Piano Concerto, K466. In the following extract Mozart plunges down an arpeggio on to the ♭IIb chord. The dramatic effect is reminiscent of the same composer's *Don Giovanni* (1787).

Mozart: Piano Concerto No. 20 in D minor, K466, 1st movt (1785)

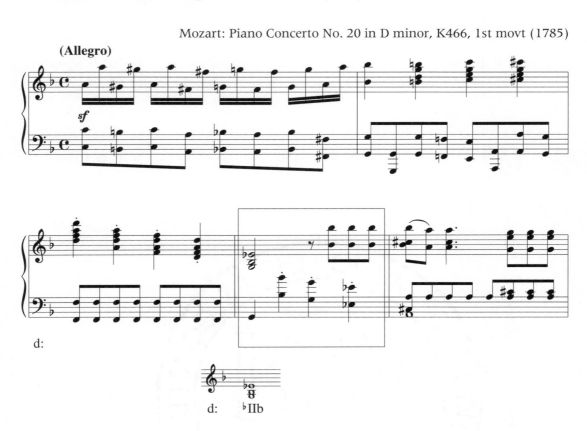

The resolution of the Neapolitan 6th

◆ Being an altered version of chord ii°, the Neapolitan 6th acts as an approach chord to V, especially at a cadence.

Beethoven: Piano Sonata in C♯ minor, Op. 27 No. 2 (1801)

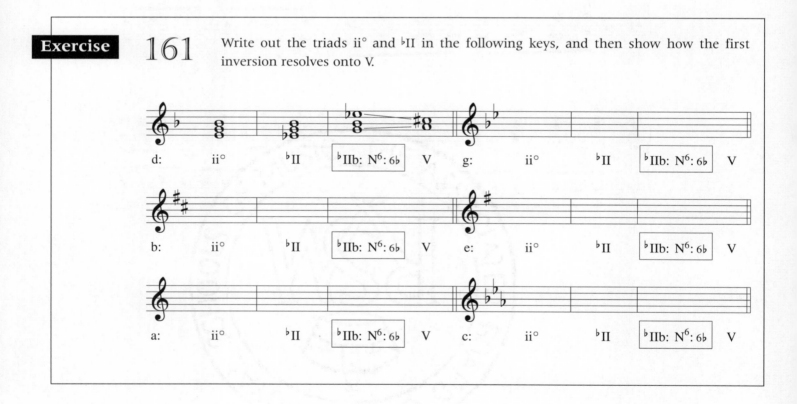

Since the chord is always referred to as the *flattened supertonic*, the labelling ♭IIb is used in all keys, whatever the notation, i.e. this D major chord is labelled ♭IIb and not ♮IIb .

Exercise 161   Write out the triads ii° and ♭II in the following keys, and then show how the first inversion resolves onto V.

◆ ♭IIb may move to Ic–V (the cadential $\frac{6}{4}$). Notice the ringed, expressive dissonances in this extract.

Mozart: Piano Concerto No. 23 in A, K488 (1786)

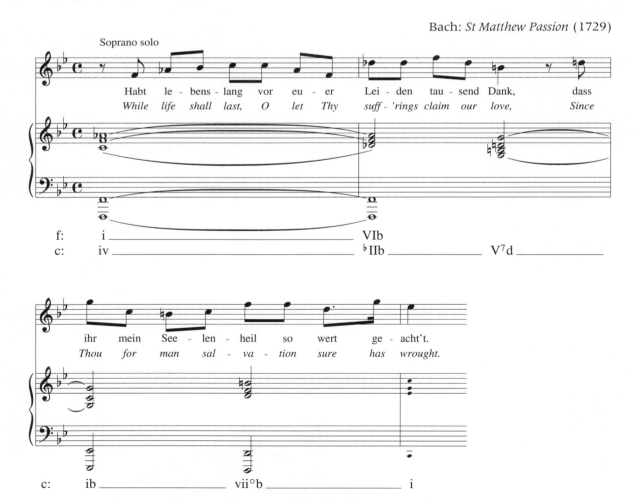

◆ ♭IIb may move onto V⁷d, vii^d7 or other chords of the dominant family.

In the following example the ♭IIb of C minor acts as a pivot chord in modulating from F minor. VIb of F minor becomes the Neapolitan 6th of C minor, and the F in the bass is held as a pedal beneath V⁷d in a cadence that confirms the change of key.

Bach: *St Matthew Passion* (1729)

◆ Before ♭IIb progresses to a chord of the dominant family it may pass to ♯iv^{d7}.

◆ Notice how the altered chords (♭IIb and ♯iv^{d7}) increase the poignancy of cadential progressions.

Mozart: Fantasia in C minor, K475 (1785)

The following exercises will help you to become familiar with the various resolutions of the Neapolitan 6th chord.

◆ In four-part writing the **bass** note of the Neapolitan 6th is normally doubled. Composers tend **not** to double the **altered** note(s) in a chord.

Exercise 162   Complete the following extracts in four parts to show the various progressions involving the Neapolitan 6th. Play or sing the examples.

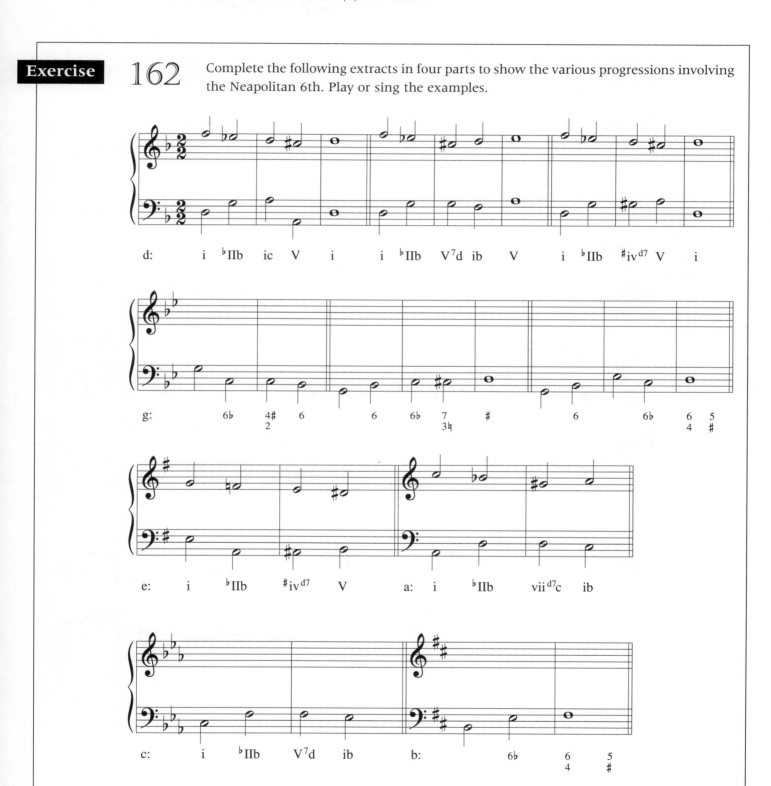

Chord ♭II

◆ In the nineteenth century the Neapolitan 6th would sometimes appear as ♭II, i.e. in root position.

In this Chopin Prelude, ♭II is preceded by VI as part of the progression of 5ths:

Chopin: Prelude in C minor, Op. 28 No. 20 (1836–9)

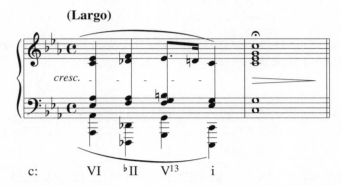

◆ Composers sometimes dwelt on ♭II so as to suggest an excursion into that key.

In the following example chord VI (G) of the tonic key, B minor, becomes the dominant 7th of C – ♭II in B minor.

Chopin: Prelude in B minor, Op. 28 No. 6 (1836–9)

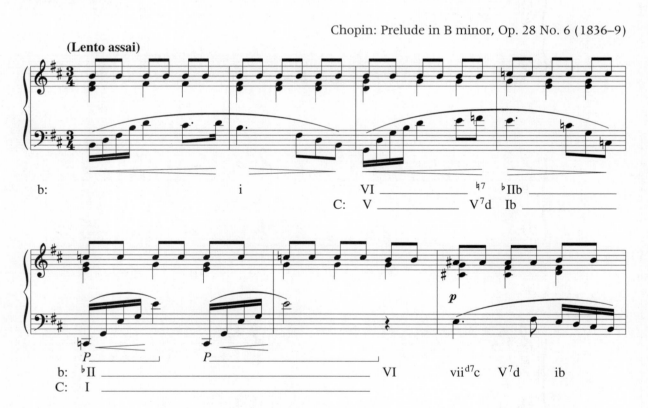

The augmented 6th chord

◆ There are several different kinds of augmented 6th, and they are all inversions of chromatically altered chords. Their distinguishing feature is the interval of the **augmented 6th**, which normally moves by semitones to the dominant notes of the key. Your quickest access to this chord may be to **start** with the dominant notes of the key and to build the augmented 6th interval on the semitones either side of those notes.

◆ The augmented 6th chord is usually built on the flattened 6th of the key.[†]
◆ For reasons unknown, the various versions of the chord have been given geographical names to distinguish one from another. Two of the chords, the **Italian** and **German**, are altered versions of chord IV. The **French 6th** is an altered version of chord ii.

Resolution

◆ As we have seen, chords ii and IV, in their diatonic versions, move naturally towards V. The chromatic inflections of the augmented 6th chords increase the strength of the progression through semitone movement towards V or Ic–V and a cadence.
◆ It helps to learn the figured bass to identify the variety of augmented 6th.

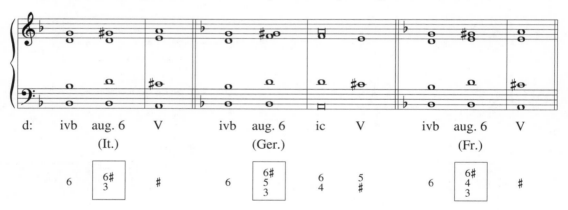

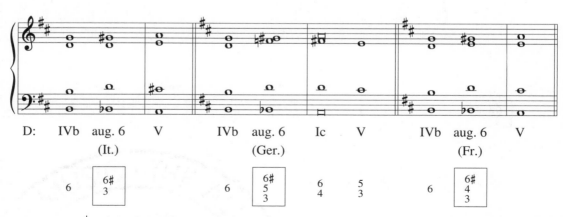

[†] Augmented 6th chords are sometimes based on other notes in the key. The closing bars of Schubert's String Quintet in C, for example, has an augmented 6th chord built on the flattened 2nd. It resolves on the tonic chord.

◆ In isolation the German 6th sounds like a dominant 7th (*a*). However, its 'spelling' and context indicate different melodic movement, outwards (*b*).

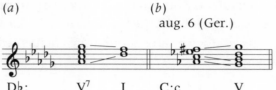

Exercises 163 Play through the following extract. Label the harmony, noting the augmented 6th chord at the two imperfect cadences.

164 On one stave, write out the augmented 6th chords and their resolutions as indicated. Use the figuring to help you.

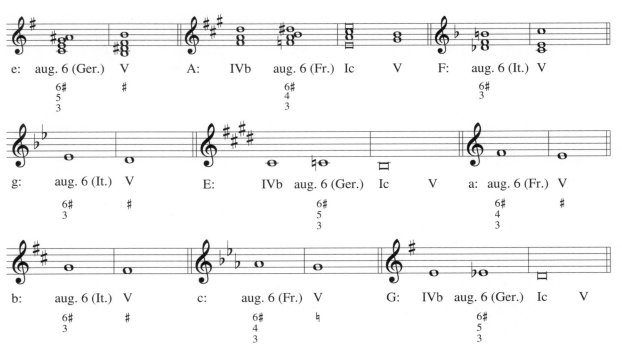

165 Complete these progressions containing augmented 6th chords. Remember that altered notes in these chords should not be doubled.

166   Complete and resolve these augmented 6th chords. Add figuring.

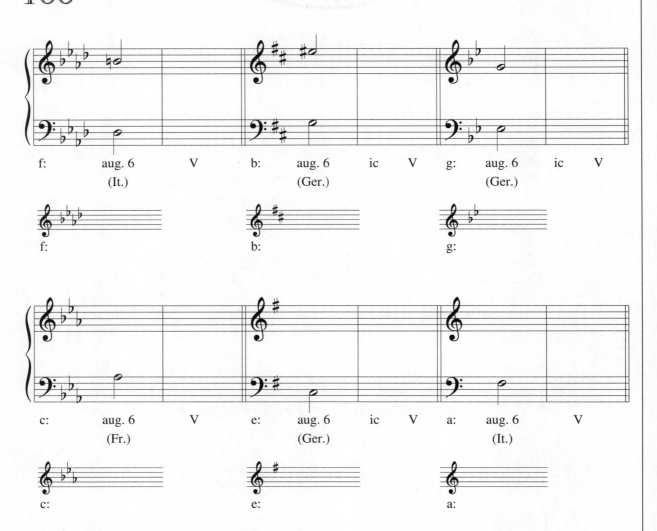

167   Study and play these examples. Figure the augmented 6th chords marked with an asterisk and show their variety.

Mozart: Piano Sonata in F, K494 (1786)

Mozart: Piano Concerto No. 20 in D minor, K466 (1785)

Beethoven: Piano Sonata in F♯, Op. 78 (1805)

Beethoven: Symphony No. 5 in C minor, Op. 67 (1807–8)

Extending the triad – 7ths, 9ths, 11ths, 13ths

◆ In Chapter 6 we saw how the 7th became an integral part of the dominant sound during the late Classical period of Haydn, Mozart and Beethoven. In that chapter we also saw how 9ths, 11ths and 13ths can be added to triads, especially the dominant. By the nineteenth century composers were freely using such extended chords, which often arose out of the melodic movement of strands in the texture.

◆ These extensions can appear in their major and minor forms.

◆ Normally, when a chord consists of a 9th, 11th or 13th, the 7th is also included

◆ Chords of the 11th are comparatively rare. When they occur, however, the 3rd of the chord is usually omitted, to avoid the semitone clash with the 11th, as in the chord marked * below.

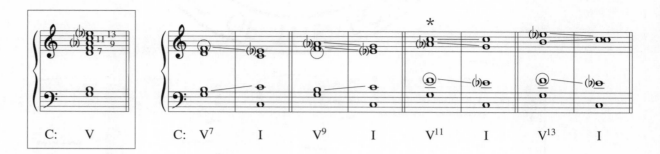

Resolutions

◆ The 7th and 9th normally move down.

◆ When not used as an appoggiatura the dominant 11th usually remains on the same note, the tonic.

◆ When not used as an appoggiatura the 13th normally falls a 3rd.

Schumann: Piano Quintet in E♭, Op. 44 (1842)

◆ When used melodically these extensions are often indistinguishable from other decorations, such as suspensions and appoggiaturas. There are exceptions, but they normally resolve down by step.

Exercises

168

Write out the following chords as extended triads.

Ab: V⁹   f#:   V¹³   g: V¹¹   D: V⁹   Bb: V¹³

e: V⁹b   b: V¹³   a: V¹¹   Eb: V¹³b   F: V⁹

d: V⁹   f: V¹³   c: V⁹   A: V⁹b   E: V¹¹

169

Label and resolve the following chords.

c: V¹³   i   D: Bb:

d: g: e:

A: B: Ab:

170

Play the following examples. Identify the chords marked with an asterisk as 7ths, 9ths, 11ths or 13ths. Notice that several are melodic decorations, such as appoggiaturas.

Schubert: Symphony No. 8 in B minor (1822)

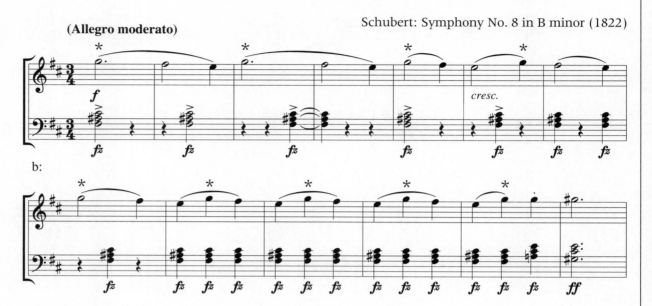

Purcell: 'When I am laid in earth',
from *Dido and Aeneas* (1689)

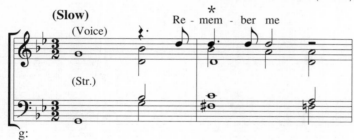

Wagner: *Götterdämmerung* (1876)

Tchaikovsky: Symphony No. 6 in B minor, Op. 74, 'Pathétique' (1893)

Mahler: Symphony No. 2, 'Resurrection', 5th movt (rev. 1893–5)

'Prepare yourself to live!'

Walton: 'Touch her soft lips and part', from the film music for *Henry V* (1944)

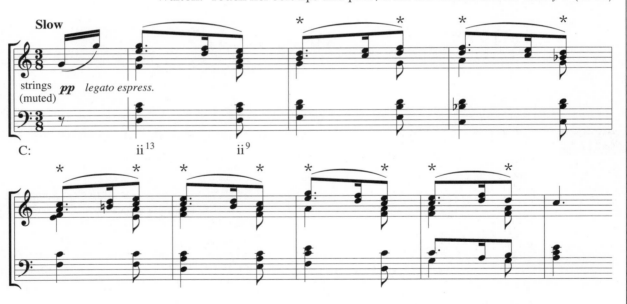

Altered notes in extended chords

◆ Extended chords often contain altered notes as well. In the following example Beethoven increases the dramatic impact by writing a minor 9th in a major key.

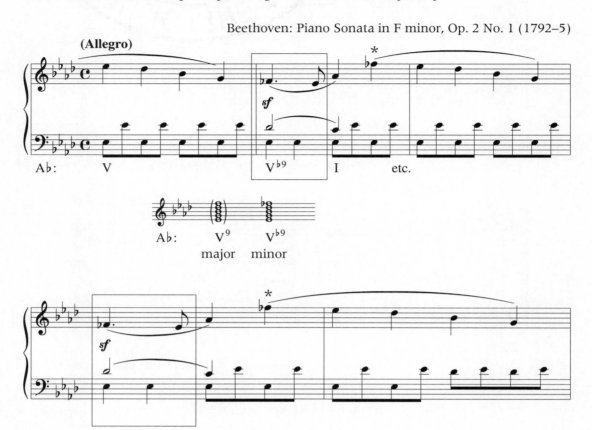

Beethoven: Piano Sonata in F minor, Op. 2 No. 1 (1792–5)

Exercises 171 Label the chords in this extract, noting the altered extended chords. Notice that Tchaikovsky introduces minor 9ths into his major melody.

Tchaikovsky: *Romeo and Juliet* (1880)

172 Identify the chords in this passage, and indicate any alterations in your label. Ring and identify any dissonances. Notice that this beautiful passage is based on a progression of fifths.

Fauré: 'Après un rêve' (1865)

'In a slumber enchanted by your image,
I was dreaming of happiness, that radiant mirage.'

Chromatic movement

◆ Traditionally, music that had descending chromatic lines in the outer parts, especially the bass line, was thought to evoke or suggest the sorrowful emotions (*see* Introduction to Part 5). In his *A Plaine and Easie Introduction to Practicall Musicke* (1597), Morley wrote 'but when you would express a lamentable passion, then must you use motions proceeding by half-notes [semitones]'.

◆ The pace of the music is also a factor in the emotional effect. In the same book Morley wrote 'if it be lamentable, the note must go in slow and heavy motions'.

There are many examples in music reaching back to the Renaissance where slow chromatic music conveys a 'lamentable passion'. In the Baroque period, a descending chromatic ground bass was regarded as particularly effective. The following ground bass creates chromatic movement in the other parts, complemented by suspensions (figured) and diminished 7ths (boxed).

Bach: 'Crucifixus', from Mass in B minor (*c.*1747–9)

'And [he] was crucified…'

◆ Such chromatic lines usually descend through only the upper **tetrachord** (four notes) of the scale.

◆ This is the ground bass for the aria 'When I am laid in earth', sung by Dido in the closing section of Purcell's *Dido and Aeneas* (1689):

Purcell: 'When I am laid in earth',
from *Dido and Aeneas* (1689)

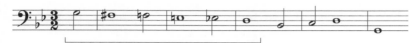

◆ The notes of a chromatic scale in the bass can be harmonized in a number of ways, such as:
- by changing the harmony from major to minor (in *Exercise 173* (*a*) below);
- by introducing a passing modulation (*Exercise 173* (*b*));
- by using chromatic chords, such as the augmented 6th (*Exercise 173* (*c*)).

◆ Lines moving chromatically **upwards** create a similar impression (*Exercise 173* (*c*)).

173 Consider the following passages and fill in the alto and tenor parts. Play them in different keys.

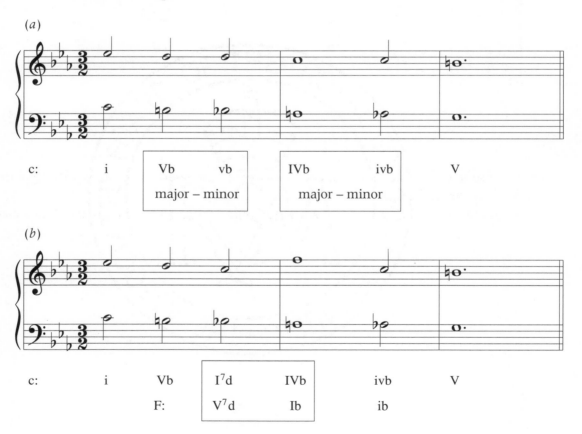

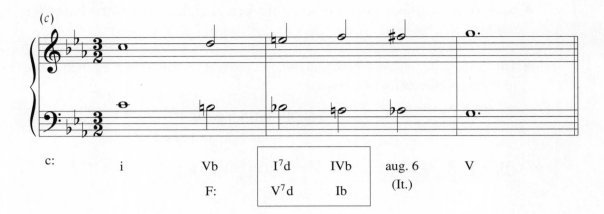

174 Consider the effect of the chromatic lines in this chorus from Handel's *Messiah* (1742).
1 Bracket the chromatic movement.
2 Label the chords.
3 Sing or play the extract.

Handel: 'Since by man came death', from *Messiah* (1742)

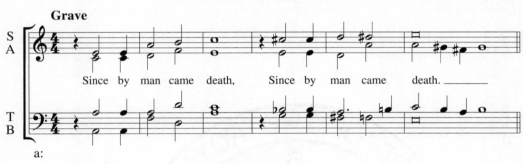

◆ Because of the semitone movement, chromatic music offers the composer the opportunity:
- to modulate freely;
- to use coloured chords, such as the Neapolitan 6th, augmented 6th and diminished 7th;
- to use cross-relations.

Exercises   175   Purcell's chilly evocation of winter in *The Fairy Queen* uses
1   chromatic movement in both directions,
2   a diminished 7th,
3   a suspension,
4   cross-relations,
5   a slow dissonant passing note, and
6   an augmented 6th chord

all in the space of nine bars!

Identify these features and number them.

Purcell: 'Winter', from *The Fairy Queen* (1692)

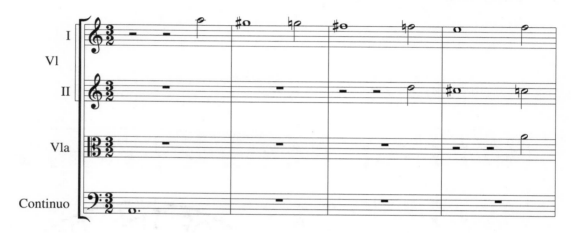

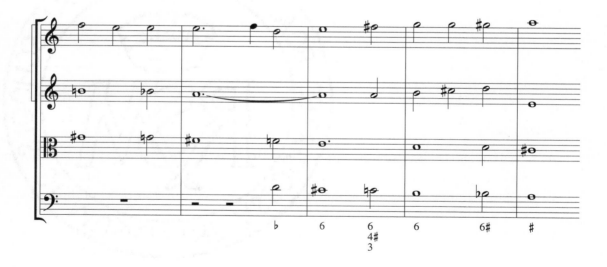

About 130 years later Chopin uses similar devices to convey emotion in his Prelude in C minor. The chromatic lines of bars 5 and 6 echo the mood of Purcell's music, including using an augmented 6th (marked *).

176

1 Play through the prelude.
2 Identify the modulations.
3 Label the circled chords.
4 Label the harmony over the descending chromatic scale.
5 Ring an appoggiatura.

Chopin: Prelude in C minor, Op. 28 No. 20 (1836–9)

Summary

As set out in the Introduction to Part 5, pages 197–8, when dissonance, chromatic movement and harmonic decoration are **combined**, we may expect music of considerable intensity and expression. Pace, texture and instrumentation may also contribute to the overall effect of the music.

Consider these various elements when playing or listening to the following extracts.

Exercises *177* Comment on the bars in brackets.

Mozart: String Quintet in G minor, K516 (1787)

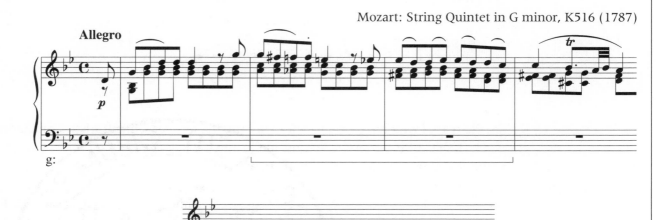

Brahms: Intermezzo, Op. 116 No. 6 (1882)

178 Play or listen to the following piece from Schumann's *Kinderszenen*. The composer seems to be searching, both melodically and harmonically, for the right version of the opening phrase.

He rejects various solutions before finding the answer which satisfies him, at bar 22.

1 Bracket the various solutions, indicating the key of each.
2 Label the chords marked with an asterisk.

Schumann: 'Träumerei', from *Kinderszenen*, Op. 15 (1838)

179   Play or listen to the opening of this haunting nocturne.

1   Label the harmony, indicating the modulations. There are two chord changes per bar, with the bass notes of the harmony sustained by the pedal.

◆ The harmony is based on the progression of 5ths, including some altered chords; tonic and dominant harmonies seem to contain the restless flight of the right hand (bars 11–15).

◆ The melodic line is also decorated, with intricate arabesques including some poignant dissonances.

2   Identify the circled notes as the following:
   a   accented passing notes,
   b   suspensions,
   c   appoggiaturas,
   d   accented auxiliary notes, or
   e   cross-relations.

Chopin: Nocturne, Op. 48 No. 1 (1837)

180   Listen carefully to this intermezzo in A major by Brahms.

In the repeat of the opening eight bars (A2) the composer alters various chords and adds dissonant decorations, creating a more expressive effect.

1. Identify the altered or extended chords in boxes. They are reduced on to one stave below the music.
2. Circle and label any dissonances in bars 11–16 (Remember that retardation is the name often given to the upward-resolving suspension.)
3. Label the harmony of bars 1–8.
4. Indicate any modulation.

Brahms: Intermezzo, Op. 118 No. 2 (1893)

Select Bibliography

COOKE, DERYCK The Language of Music (OUP, 1959)

CROCKER, RICHARD A History of Musical Style (McGraw-Hill, 1966)

HUTCHINGS, ARTHUR The Invention and Composition of Music (Novello, 1958)

KEYS, IVOR The Texture of Music from Purcell to Brahms (Dennis Dobson, 1961)

LEDBETTER, DAVID Continuo Playing According to Handel (OUP, 1990)

OTTMAN, ROBERT Advanced Harmony (Prentice-Hall Inc., N.J., 1961)

ROSEN, CHARLES The Classical Style (Faber & Faber, 1971)

SHUMWAY, STANLEY Harmony and Ear Training at the Keyboard (McGraw-Hill, 1984)

STEINITZ, PAUL AND STERMAN, STELLA Harmony in Context (Belwin-Mills Music, 1976)

Index of Composers

Page numbers in roman type are quotations, in **bold** type exercises, and those preceded by an asterisk are textual references.

Adams, J. (b. 1947) *xiiin
Arne, T. (1710–78) **111**

Bach, C. P. E. (1714–88) **122**, **216**
Bach, J. S. (1685–1750) **15**, 17, *18, *20, *33, 38, *38, 39, 40, 50, 54, 56, *57, **58**, 75, 76, **76**, 80, **81**, 82, **86**, 87, **89**, *90, **94**, **95**, 96, **96**, **99**, **101**, 107, **108**, *110, **120**, *125, **127**, **129**, **130**, **131**, **132**, *132, **135**, **136**, 137, **138**, 142, 143, **144**, 145, **146**, **152**, **153**, 153, **155**, 156, **157**, **158**, **159**, **160**, 166, 168, **174**, 177, **177–8**, *180, 181, **182**, **183**, **184**, *191, 192, 199–200, 204, **206**, **207**, **208**, 209, 212, 218, **219**, **220**, **221**, **222**, **223**, **225**, **228**, **229**, **236**, 237, 239, 254
Bartók, B. (1881–1945) *xii
Beethoven, L. van (1770–1827) *xi, *33, *37, 38, 52, **55**, **56**, **78**, 83, 84, **85**, *90, 106, **109**, **123**, **152**, **156**, 163, 164, **164–5**, 166–7, 175, 176, **181–2**, **190**, *191, 195, **236**, 238, **244**, **247**, *247, 252
Bennet, J. (c.1575–c.1614) 208
Berlioz, H. (1803–69) *xii, **236**
Böhm, G. (1661–1733) **112**
Boulez, P. (b. 1925) *xiiin
Brahms, J. (1833–97) *26n, *33, **140**, *172, 173, **215**, **259**, **264**
Britten, B. (1913–76) *xii
Buxtehude, D. (c.1637–1707) **78**
Byrd, W. (1543–1623) *39, 199

Caccini, G. (c.1545–1618) *xi
Casson, M. (c.1795) **61**
Chopin, F. (1810–49) 124, 202, **205**, **227**, 242, *257, **258**, **262–3**
Clarke, J. (c.1674–1707) 110
Clérambault, L.-N. (1676–1749) 121
Copland, A. (1900–90) *xii
Corelli, A. (1653–1713) *xi, 27, **28**, 57, 77, **133**, **134**, **158**, 200–01, 210, *218, 221, **226**
Couperin, L. (c.1626–61) *110, **112**
Croft, W. (1678–1727) 127, **178**

Debussy, C. (1862–1918) *xii, 17, *33, 34, *36, 37

Dowland, J. (1563–1626) **36**, **88**
Dunstable, J. (c.1390–1453) *202

Elgar, E. (1857–1934) 106, **159**, 191

Fauré, G. (1845–1924) 87, **253**

Glass, P. (b. 1937) *xiiin

Handel, G. F. (1685–1759) 18, **26–7**, **28**, **78**, **95**, 95, 104, *110, 120, **122**, *125, **152**, **160**, **256**
Haydn, J. (1732–1809) *xi, **15**, 16, 18, **78**, **99**, 108, 169, 195, 230, *247
Hindemith, P. (1895–1963) xi
Hook, J. (1746–1827) **61**
Humperdinck, E. (1854–1921) **193**

Janáček, L. (1854–1928) *xii
Jones, R. (d. 1744) 119

Lawes, H. (1596–1662) **88**, **160**
Leisentritt, J. (1527–86) **124**
Liszt, F. (1811–86) *59, 124
Lully, J.-B. (1632–87) *208
Luther, M. (1483–1546) **129**

Mahler, G. (1860–1911) *59, **251**
Mendelssohn, F. (1809–47) **15**, **44**, **224**, 233
Messiaen, O. (1908–92) *xii
Monteverdi, C. (1567–1643) *xi, *217
Morley, T. (1557/8–1602) *33, *254
Mozart, L. (1719–87) ix
Mozart, W. A. (1756–91) *xi, **14**, 18, **28**, 40, *51, 52, **54**, **55**, *88, **89**, *90, 91–2, 97, **97**, **98**, **100**, **101**, **102**, 104–5, 108, **109**, 110, **113–14**, **123**, **127**, **128**, **138**, 143, *146, 147, **188**, *189, 189, *193, 194, *195, 201, **205**, **209**, **211**, **212**, **216**, **217**, 223, **224**, **226–7**, 233, 237, 239, 240, **246**, **247**, *247, **259**

Palestrina, G. P. (1525–94) 27
Petzold, C. (1677–1733) **101**, 110
Praetorius, M. (c.1571–1621) **22**
Purcell, H. (1659–95) *xi, *40, 81,

87, *88, **89**, *110, **155**, **185**, 197–8, **208**, 224, **231**, **250**, 255, **257**

Ravel, M. (1875–1937) **141**
Ravenscroft, T. (c.1582–c.1635) **36**, **128**, **179**
Reich, S. (b. 1936) *xiiin
Reinhardt, K. (1710/11–67) **125**
Rossini, G. (1792–1868) 51
Rouget de Lisle, C.-J. (1760–1836) 143

Scarlatti, A. (1660–1725) *236
Scarlatti, D. (1685–1757) *110
Schoenberg, A. (1874–1951) *xii
Schubert, F. (1797–1828) 17, 69, **70**, 106, **139**, 146, 169–70, **173**, **180**, 187, *191, 191, *243n, **250**
Schumann, R. (1810–56) **70**, 71, **144**, **180**, **213–14**, 248, **252**, **260–61**
Shostakovich, D. (1906–75) *xii, **89**
Stölzel, G. (1690–1749) **186**
Strauss, R. (1864–1949) *106
Stravinsky, I. (1882–1971) *xii
Sullivan, A. (1842–1900) **44**
Sweelinck, J. (1562–1621) **155**

Tallis, T. (c.1505–85) *39, 39, 127
Tchaikovsky, P. (1840–93) **71**, **141**, **156**, 179, **251**
Telemann, G. (1681–1767) **111**
Tomkins, T. (1572–1656) 222
Triller, V. (d. c.1573) **124**

Verdi, G. (1813–1901) 168
Vivaldi, A. (1678–1741) *63, 63, 117, **121**, **126**, *127, *218

Wagner, R. (1813–83) *52, 194, *195, **250**
Walton, W. (1902–83) **251**
Weber, C. (1786–1826) 85
Weelkes, T. (c.1576–1623) 39, 88
Weiss, S. (1686–1750) **131**
Wesley, S. (1766–1837) 174

General Index

Page references in **bold** type indicate main entries.